Understanding, Measuring, and Improving Daily Management

How to Use Effective Daily Management to Drive Significant Process Improvement

T0293513

Understanding, Measuring, and Improving Daily Management

How to Use Effective Daily Management to Drive Significant Process Improvement

By
Ross Kenneth Kennedy

Routledge
Taylor & Francis Group

A PRODUCTIVITY PRESS BOOK

First edition published in 2019
by Routledge/Productivity Press
711 Third Avenue New York, NY 10017, USA
2 Park Square, Milton Park, Abingdon, Oxon OX14 4RN, UK

Printed in Canada on acid-free paper

International Standard Book Number-13: 978-1-138-58941-4 (Hardback)
International Standard Book Number-13: 978-1-138-58928-5 (Paperback)
International Standard Book Number-13: 978-0-429-49167-2 (eBook)

Library of Congress Cataloging-in-Publication Data

Names: Kennedy, Ross Kenneth, author. Title: Understanding, measuring, and improving daily management: how to use effective daily management to drive significant process improvement/Ross Kenneth Kennedy.
Description: Boca Raton: Taylor & Francis, 2019. | Includes bibliographical references and index.
Identifiers: LCCN 2018034656 (print) | LCCN 2018040031 (ebook) | ISBN 9780429491672 (e-Book) |
ISBN 9781138589414 | ISBN 9781138589414(hardback :alk. paper) | ISBN 9781138589285(paperback:alk. paper)
Subjects: LCSH: Total quality management. | Organizational effectiveness. Classification: LCC HD62.15 (ebook) |
LCC HD62.15 .K46 2019 (print) | DDC 658.4—dc23 LC record available at https://lccn.loc.gov/2018034656

Visit the Taylor & Francis Web site at
http://www.taylorandfrancis.com

Contents

Introduction: The Importance of Effective Daily Management

Role of Effective Daily Management in Achieving Operational Excellence

To achieve Operational Excellence, organisations need a continuous improvement strategy that includes reactive improvement, a stable Production or Work Plan through flow logic, and pro-active improvement. Unfortunately, many organisations get so focused on pro-active improvement through their Lean, Six Sigma, TPM (Total Production Maintenance) or Operational Excellence initiatives that they lose sight of the importance of reactive improvement and having a stable Production or Work Plan (Figure 0.1).

Reactive improvement is focused on running the business through effective daily management whereas Pro-active improvement is focused on improving the business by achieving your improvement vision. Creating a stable Production or Work Plan through flow logic enables reactive improvement and pro-active improvement to proceed with minimal disruptions caused by fire-fighting throughout the supply chain as Production or Work Plans are unexpectedly getting changed.

We have found if reactive improvement or stability is poor, you may struggle to find time for pro-active improvement. As the pro-active improvement journey

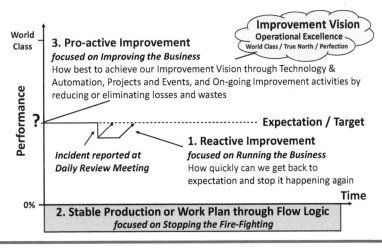

Figure 0.1 The three critical parts of a continuous improvement strategy.

can take many years to achieve Operational Excellence, there is a strong argument for getting effective daily management through reactive improvement in place sooner rather than later.

This is best demonstrated in Figures 0.2 and 0.3 which outline the impact of different approaches when trying to achieve Operational Excellence.

The first approach recognises the importance of having effective daily management through properly deployed reactive improvement supported by progressively stabilising the Production or Work Plan using such methods as the Glenday Sieve and Flow Logic. As the Production or Work Plan stabilises and daily management improves, there is more time available for everyone to work on pro-active improvement resulting in achieving Operational Excellence within a realistic timeframe.

Sadly, the second approach of poor prioritising of the three critical parts of a continuous improvement strategy is what we find at many organisations where the focus is on applying all the pro-active improvement tools with little work on stabilising the Production or Work Plan or having effective daily management. As a result of this, after many years little progress has been made in achieving the Operational Excellence targets that other best practice or world class organisations achieve because everyone is too busy responding to urgent day-to-day issues that keep reoccurring, or they are fire-fighting as the Production or Work Plan regularly gets unexpectedly changed.

Hence effective daily management through reactive improvement is a critical foundation for achieving Operational Excellence.

Why Reactive Improvement Is Important

Too often we find sites obsessed with trying to achieve new production records in an attempt to increase overall output. The sad reality is that trying to achieve

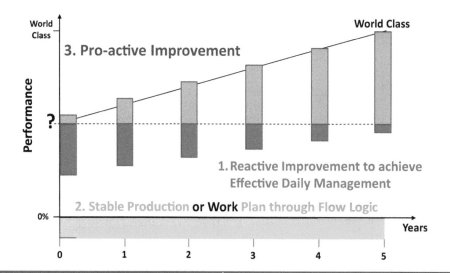

Figure 0.2 **Effective prioritising of the three critical parts of a continuous improvement strategy.**

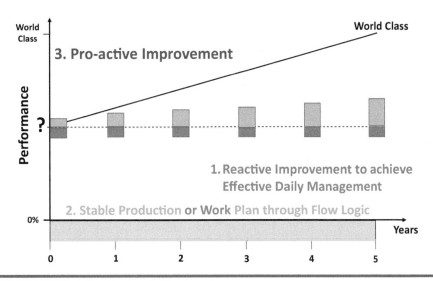

Figure 0.3   Poor prioritising of the three critical parts of a continuous improvement strategy.

new production records rather than focusing on why the average or target performance was not achieved will nearly always lead to less total output over the longer term such as a 12-month period.

Chasing new production records may sound very heroic and may create great motivation within the workforce, especially if linked to attractive rewards or bonuses; however, when compared to the long-term average performance that can be achieved through reactive improvement, the difference can be quite significant.

As highlighted in Figure 0.4, chasing production records will often widen the distribution curve as there is often very poor performance after a record has been achieved, because the plant has been pushed too hard resulting in unforeseen failures or disruptions.

By reviewing performance daily, by shift, and by the hour, and putting the effort into why the desired (average or target) performance was not achieved and rapidly identifying and addressing the root causes, you will progressively reduce the variation in performance and move the distribution curve to the right, increasing the average and resulting in a greater output over the long term along with significant lower costs.

What Is Reactive Improvement?

Reactive improvement develops the capability and discipline within the organisation to be able to rapidly recover from an event or incident that stops you from achieving your expected or target performance for the day, shift or hour and most importantly, your ability to capture the learning and initiate corrective actions so that the event or incident will not reoccur anywhere across the organisation.

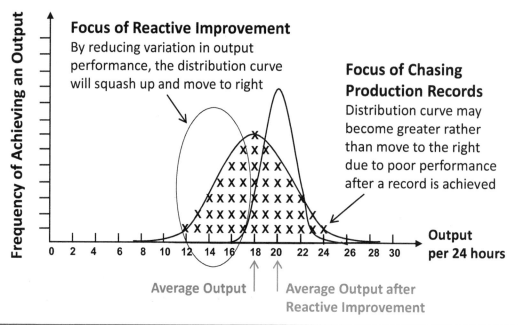

Figure 0.4 Impact of reactive improvement compared to chasing production records.

As such, reactive improvement focuses on improving daily management through your Daily Review Meetings, your information centres supporting the Daily Review Meetings and your Frontline Problem-Solving Root Cause Analysis capability at all levels, especially at the frontline.

The Seven Key Elements of Reactive Improvement

There are seven key elements of reactive improvement that need to work in concert for effective daily management:

1. **Supportive organisation structure** to support development of your people so they have ownership and accountability for the performance of their area of responsibility;
2. **Effective Frontline Leaders** to ensure everyone else in the leadership structure are not working down a level;
3. **Appropriate measures** with expected targets that are linked to the site's Key Success Factors for Operations to ensure goal alignment, and are relevant to the area being focused on;
4. **Structured Daily Review Meetings** to identify opportunities (problems/ incidents) and monitor progress of their solution so they don't happen again;
5. **Visual Information Centres** that visually display daily and trending performance along with monitoring of actions to address problems/issues raised;

6. **Frontline Problem-Solving Root Cause Analysis capability** across the site; and
7. **Rapid sharing of learning capability** across shifts, departments and the organisation.

Determine Your Starting Point

On the next page is an Effective Daily Management Innocence to Excellence Rating Sheet allowing you to score your department or site to establish a starting point or baseline to monitor the impact of your reactive improvement activities. The rating sheet covers the seven elements identified above.

For each of the five lines in the seven elements, please score your department or site 1 to 10 using the words in the appropriate block as a guide for your rating, i.e. if the words in the first block described your perception of your department or site, you would rate between 0 and 3 depending on how close the words described your perception. If, however, the words in the second block better reflected your perception you would rate between 3 and 7. If, however, the words in the third block better reflected your perception you would rate between 7 and 10.

Once you score each element, total each of the element scores (out of a possible 50) then multiply it by 2 and divide by 10 to give you a score out of 10 which is entered in the space provided on the rating sheet. These scores are then added to give a total score (out of possible 70). This total score can be divided by 7 and multiplied by 10 to give you a percentage score (out of possible 100). A spreadsheet to collate the scores can be obtained from CTPM – The Centre for Australasian TPM & Lean/CI by emailing ctpm@ctpm.org.au.

We suggest you get a range of people in your department or at your site who attend Daily Review Meetings to do the rating so your baseline becomes more robust.

If your site scores below 80%, you may find the information in the remainder of this book covering the seven key elements useful in developing your reactive improvement action plans to achieve Effective Daily Management.

Innocence	Effective Daily Management Innocence to Excellence Rating							Excellence			Score
0	1	2	3	4	5	6	7	8	9	10	

1. Supportive Organisational Structure		(Score/50) × 2/10 =/10	
Production personnel are regularly moved throughout the plant with little ownership to the equipment or an area	Some production personnel work in a fixed area	Production structure based on Area Based Teams of 4–8 with designated areas of responsibility	
No designated Frontline Leaders (wages)	Frontline Leaders (wages) appointed but have more than 7 direct reports	Frontline Leader (wages) with no more than 7 direct reports	
No Frontline Leaders (wages), just senior operators who spend most of their time operating the plant	Frontline Leaders (wages) exist however poorly trained and not held accountable for achievement of plan	Frontline Leaders (wages) are competent and spend less than 50% of their time operating the plant	
Production and maintenance have independent rosters so there is no alignment	More than 50% of maintenance personnel have aligned rosters with production	Production and maintenance rosters are aligned or supportive to allow a designated maintainer to support each Production Area Based Team	
Maintenance or quality support is rarely available when requested and not sure who will turn up	Maintenance or quality support is available when requested however not sure who will turn up	Each Production Area Based Team has a designated maintainer and quality person whose rosters are aligned or supportive.	

2. Effective Frontline Leaders		(Score/50) × 2/10 =/10	
Main role is to provide technical support regarding operating the plant	Expected to ensure the work plan for their direct reports is achieved however not expected to report at a daily review meeting	Competent in achieving the daily work plan, leading a start of day/shift meeting and reporting at a Daily Review Meeting	
Can only competently operate a few work stations within their area of responsibility	Able to operate all work stations, however, relies on others for set-ups/changeovers	Competent in the set-up and operation of all work station responsible for	
Have had no training or involvement in formal improvement activities	Some involvement in formal improvement however not competent at leading such	Competent in improvement activities such as 5 S and operator equipment care	
Has no interest or skill in getting all direct reports to work as an effective team	Struggles to get direct reports to work as an effective team	Competent in team skills and developing team chemistry within their team	
Does not get involved in the formal training of their direct reports	Able to show their direct reports what to do	Competent in the training of all their direct reports	

3. Appropriate Measures (linked to Key Success Factors for Operations)		(Score/50) × 2/10 =/10	
No Key Success Factors for Operations identified	Key Success Factors for Operations identified but not prioritised in order of importance	Key Success Factors for Operations are prioritised by consensus and supported with an aspiration statement for each	
No timeframe for achieving world class performance	Timeframe identified but not shared	Timeframe for achieving world class performance clear to all	
No world class targets set for performance measures	World class targets established for some performance measures	World class targets set for all performance measures	
No definitions displayed with each performance measure	There are some definitions displayed	Clear definitions displayed with all performance measures	
No owners allocated to each Key Success Factor for Operations	Owners allocated to some Key Success Factors for Operations	Each Key Success Factor for Operations has an owner responsible to ensure all reporting is to the site standard	

4. Structured Daily Review Meetings		(Score/50) × 2/10 =/10	
Meeting rarely starts on time, and often runs over	Meeting sometimes starts and finishes on time	Meetings always start and finish on time, with full attendance at start of meetings	
No formal agenda exists and only the leader can run the meeting	Formal agenda exists but often not followed, and leader as well as only some direct reports can run the meeting	Formal agenda is always followed, and leader as well as their direct reports run the meeting on weekly rotation	
Issues are discussed, but follow-up tasks rarely allocated	Follow-up tasks are verbally allocated and personally noted	Identified tasks are noted on display board with follow-up date	
Focus is on collecting information from reports to explain performance issues	Focus of discussions is on gaining an understanding of what caused performance issues	Focus of discussions is on ensuring Frontline Leaders leave meeting fully supported to achieve Production Plan	
Held in an area full of distractions.	Held close to operations with few distractions	Stand-up meetings, close to operations area and no distractions	

Innocence				Effective Daily Management Innocence to Excellence Rating				Excellence			Score
0	1	2	3	4	5	6	7	8	9	10	

5. Visual Information Centres (where Daily Review Meeting conducted)		**(Score/50) × 2/10 =/10**	
All performance information kept in reports or on computer so meeting area has no performance information displayed on boards	Information centres established with daily performance information displayed on boards, but not to any site standard	Information centres established close to area and to site standard so all information centres are easy to interpret	
Previous day's performance is discussed verbally	Previous day's performance recorded on documents	Previous day's performance is noted on board next to target using visual standards (e.g. achieved – green; missed – red)	
Layout of information on boards is haphazard and difficult to distinguish	Layout of information on boards is well defined, but not in the order of the Key Success Factors for Operations or agenda	Easy to update information which is displayed in order of the Key Success Factors for Operations and supports agenda flow	
Poor area (noisy, cramped, distractions, no clock in room etc.)	Reasonable area (stand-up, good vision, clock in room etc.)	Excellent area (stand-up, easy to hear and see, no distractions, clock in room has visual controls to indicate start and finish time)	
Root Cause Analysis, if initiated, is done randomly (no policies)	Triggers for initiating Root Cause Analysis are displayed and generally adhered to	Up-to-date policies including triggers for initiating Root Cause Analysis are displayed, and always followed	
6. Frontline Problem-Solving Root Cause Analysis		**(Score/50) × 2/10 =/10**	
No Personnel at Daily Review Meeting trained in Root Cause Analysis to site standard	Half the personnel at Daily Review Meeting trained in Root Cause Analysis to site standard	All personnel at Daily Review Meeting trained in Frontline Problem-Solving Root Cause Analysis to site standard	
No policy in place for solving incidents or problems raised at Daily Review Meetings	Policy in place for solving incidents or problems raised at Daily Review Meetings but no formal standardised process used	Policy supported by triggers which are regularly reviewed, in place for initiating Frontline Problem-Solving Root Cause Analysis to site standard	
No timeframe targets in place for Root Cause Analysis	Some timeframe targets in place for Root Cause Analysis	Timeframe target in place for reporting back proposed solutions	
Root Cause Analysis A3 Summary Sheets not used to record analysis and outcomes	Root Cause Analysis A3 Summary Sheets sometimes used to record analysis, but not completed to a site standard or filed centrally	Once allocated, Root Cause Analysis A3 Summary Sheets are completed within agreed time to site standard, shared and filed	
No person dedicated to support and facilitate Root Cause Analysis	Random facilitation support provided for Root Cause Analysis	Formal facilitation support provided for all Root Cause Analysis	
7. Rapid Sharing of Learning		**(Score/50) × 2/10 =/10**	
Agreed standards are not seen as important as individuality is promoted – do it whichever way you feel is best	Some standards are deployed across the site however still a lot of gaps	Agreed standards are widely deployed across the site so everyone can quickly and easily understand the situation	
There is no formal CI knowledge base for collecting and disseminating previous CI activities/analysis	CI knowledge base has been established however it is on a common drive and sometimes hard to find information	A formal CI knowledge base framed around the site's equipment structure is effective and accessible by all	
There is no equipment structure established at site to capture information such as maint history etc.	Equipment Structure exists but is only used for collecting Maintenance information	A common equipment structure is used to capture maint information, CI information (CI knowledge base) and cost information	
Root Cause Analysis A3 Summary Sheets are rarely generated if at all	Root Cause Analysis A3 Summary Sheets are generated to capture learning, however, there is no site standard for describing information e.g. 'object-deviation'	There is a formal sign-off procedure for all Root Cause Analysis A3 Summary Sheets to ensure they comply to the site standard and are easy to understand by all	
Daily Review Meetings poorly attended and are ad-hoc in nature	Formal Daily Review Meetings are held at different levels however timing is not optimised to promote sharing of learning	There is a formal Daily Review Meeting plan covering all levels and departments that supports rapid learning and is rigidly followed	

Add up the seven scores to give you a Total Score:/70

Note

1. CI (continuous improvement).

Chapter 1

Supportive Organisation Structure – Element 1

There has been much written about organisational structures and span of control; however, if you are seeking to develop an Operational Excellence organisation that is based on developing the capability of all your people so they can be effective problem solvers, use Visual Management to identify problems at the earliest possible time, and practice Prevention at Source to stop problems from happening, then we need to understand the key aspects of Operational Excellence.

The first is Dr. W. Edwards Deming's three key points regarding quality, which he taught the Japanese in their formative years of developing the Toyota Production System that led to the introduction of single-piece flow.

1. **Focus on the process, not just the activity** – look at the performance of the whole line to ensure the workload is balanced rather just the activity of one person.
2. **Apply 'Prevention at Source' for the process** – ensure problems and issues are identified at the earliest possible time rather than at the end of the line after all the value has been added.
3. **Recognise the 'Tyranny of Time' when addressing problems** – the longer the time gap between when a quality problem occurs and you finding out about it, the less chance you will have of easily finding the root cause.

The cost implications of not finding quality problems at the earliest possible time can have a significant negative impact on the bottom line as outlined in Figure 1.1.

As such, your organisation structure should be designed to ensure all people with direct reports can play a leading role in assisting their direct reports to find and respond to quality problems at the earliest possible time, rather than the more traditional focus of just allocating and managing tasks.

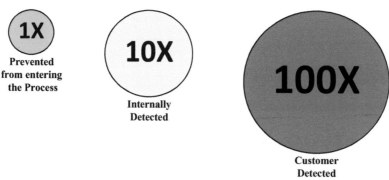

The Cost of Product Defects when they are:

1X
Prevented
from entering
the Process

10X
Internally
Detected

100X
Customer
Detected

Figure 1.1 **The cost of product defects when they are detected.**

The second is the importance of Workplace Ownership and its impact on plant and equipment reliability, more specifically stopping breakdowns and achieving best practice Overall Equipment Effectiveness (OEE) performance based on your business requirements.

The Causes of Equipment Failure and the 5 Whys

Before discussing the causes of equipment failure, we would like to refresh your memory of the improvement tool called Why-Why Analysis or the 5 Whys by Talichi Ohno.

Why-Why Analysis is a simple technique of asking why 5 times recognising that after 5 whys you are most likely to be at the root cause or primary cause for the problem.

We will use a simple example to demonstrate what we mean. A person lives in a house that has a long drive way going down to the garage under the house. One morning they get in their car to go to work and back the car out of the garage and up the long driveway only to find the car is steering funny. They could ignore this and keep driving to work (not very smart) or they could stop at the top of the driveway and ask the question:
Why (1) is the car driving funny?

They get out and investigate and find they have a flat front tyre. At this point they can curse and change the wheel and carry on OR ask the question:
Why (2) is the tyre flat?

After examining the flat tyre they discover a large nail in it. At this point they can curse a bit more and put on the spare wheel OR ask the question:
Why (3) did the tyre get a nail it?

Knowing the car didn't appear to have a flat tyre last night when it was driven home they walk down the driveway looking for nails and find several

similar nails on the garage floor. At this point they could sweep up the nails, put on the spare wheel and carry on, OR ask the question:
Why (4) were there nails on the garage floor?

Knowing they didn't put them there themself they could ask the other members of the family and discover that their children had been playing with the nails and left them on the floor. At this point they could chastise their children, sweep up the nails, put on the spare wheel and carry on, OR ask the question:
Why (5) were the children able to get hold of the nails?

They then remember they were using the nails on the weekend and left them out in easy access for the children instead of putting them away when they rushed off to watch the football on TV.

So what is the root cause? Having children! No, it's leaving the nails out so the children could get to them.

Unless the nails are properly put away, it is likely they will end up on the garage floor again.

In the workplace we rarely get to the root cause because we are too busy changing the flat tyres! However, unless we get to the root cause we will always have problems reappearing.

What Is the Pathway of Mechanical Equipment Failure?

If we work backwards from equipment failure (a bit like the 5 Why Analysis approach) and ask what indications we had that the equipment might fail, we first find *poor performance* often occurs before failure. Before this, we often have *vibration, noise, heat and/or fumes* coming from our equipment. This can be caused by one of two reasons (Figure 1.2):

1. Natural deterioration, or
2. Early or accelerated deterioration

Natural deterioration: Is when an item or component reaches its design life. Everything has a life due to normal operation. Ideally all the components should achieve their design life; however, what we find in many situations is that components deteriorate earlier than their design life.

Early or accelerated deterioration: This is where a component of the equipment wears out quicker than is expected. In other words, it wears out quicker than its design life. Its life is shortened because its natural deterioration is accelerated. This is the area of focus that can save significant costs if we are able to reduce or eliminate early or accelerated deterioration. To understand more about this, let us look at failure mechanisms.

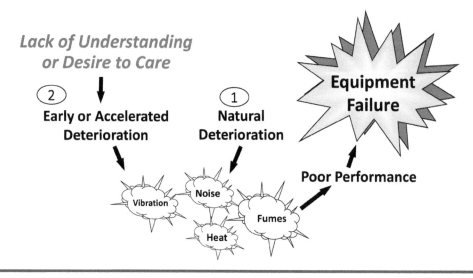

Figure 1.2 **Indicators of pending mechanical equipment failure.**

Failure Mechanisms of the Parts that Make Up Our Plant and Equipment

Failure Mechanisms

To simplify the discussion, let us look at the failure mechanisms of the mechanical parts that make up our plant and equipment. A simple example we use in our workshops is the laptop computer or data projector which is sitting in front of everyone. The parts of a laptop computer or data projector, like most pieces of equipment in our plants, can be broken down into three broad categories:

1. **Structural Items** such as the casing or housing
2. **Wear Items** such as the keyboard
3. **Working Items** which are all the moving parts like the switches, fan, etc. that make the laptop or data projector function

In Table 1.1 we have identified the different failure mechanisms for the three different categories of items.

Our main interest is with the working items. These by far make up the majority of items which need maintenance attention and often contribute most to our overall Maintenance Spend. So, let us understand the impact of the laws of physics on our working parts.

Table 1.1 **Failure Mechanisms**

	Structural Items	*Wear Items*	*Working Items*
Part	Frame Housing Casing	Wear plates Pump impellers Table rolls	Gearboxes Pumps Motors
Failure Mechanisms	Corrosion Erosion Fatigue Damage	Dependant on throughput Note: the higher the OEE, the shorter the life	Governed by the laws of physics

Example of the Impact of the Laws of Physics on the Failure Mechanisms of Working Items

- Movement between contacting surfaces creates friction and wear
- Proper lubrication provides an interface between moving surfaces
- A key role of lubrication is to be a sacrificial wear element.

Hence early or accelerated deterioration occurs when:

- Lubrication is not present
- Lubrication is incorrect for the application
- Lubrication between the surfaces is forced out due to overload
- Lubrication wears out
- Lubrication becomes contaminated

If we were to rub our hands together for the rest of the day we will get very sore hands because the layers of skin rub off. To stop this from happening we would need to apply some form of lubrication to act as an interface between our hands.

Proper lubrication provides an interface between moving surfaces and a key role of lubrication is to be a sacrificial wear element. That is, the lubrication wears out as the moving surfaces interface with it. This is why we are recommended to replace the oil in our cars at say every 10,000 km. This is not because the oil is dirty even though it may look dirty; it is continuously filtered and clean. The reason for replacement is that the oil has worn out.

Hence, as an example, 'early or accelerated deterioration' occurs when lubrication is not present, lubrication is incorrect for the application, lubrication between surfaces is forced out due to overload, lubrication wears out or lubrication becomes contaminated.

Often when walking through business plants we see operators 'blow down' the equipment with compressed air, or hose it down with high-pressure water so as to get rid of contamination, such as spillage. Unfortunately, what most operators don't understand is that they could be forcing contamination into the sensitive parts of the equipment, such as bearing seals or electrical cabinets, without even realising it or caring about it. In other words, *lack of understanding* or *desire to care* is the primary cause of early or accelerated deterioration.

We have found that the lack of understanding or desire to care can come from many sources including:

Designing
Procuring and Storing
Installing
Operating
Maintaining

We have also found that, apart from new plants where design problems often abound, the biggest issue in existing plants is often the lack of understanding or desire to care in the way we operate the plant.

As mentioned earlier, who has ever seen an operator 'blow down' the equipment with compressed air, or hose it down with water? Why do they do it? They either don't understand the implications or they couldn't give a damn/bugger – their supervisor told them to keep the place clean so this is the quickest way.

If we acknowledge there is a need to stop early or accelerated deterioration, then our challenge is how we do this.

Our learning has been that it all has to do with 'ownership'.

We have found that if people have a sense of ownership for something they will tend to take more care with it than if they don't have a sense of ownership.

For example, think about the vehicles purchased or leased by your company. Many companies have common-use vehicles on site such as a company ute or pick-up, as well as having managers who have a vehicle allocated to them.

In most cases, both are company assets from reputable suppliers, yet after a year or so we often find there is quite a significant difference in their running costs and re-sale value. The most common reason for this is based on this issue of ownership. In the majority of cases, because the manager has perceived ownership of the vehicle he or she will care for the vehicle, that is, ensure it is regularly serviced and any problems are addressed as soon as practical. With the company ute or pick-up, most people using it tend not to care or take responsibility for its condition.

The impact is often a significant difference in the running costs, performance and the resale value of these vehicles.

We find in most situations the manager's car has lower running costs and higher re-sale value.

At one mine site several years ago in Queensland we were running our 2-day workshop. The service manager made the comment that he had recently completed a review of the running costs of the company utes compared to the company cars used by managers and the figures came out: Car: 7 c/km; Ute: 67 c/km due to all the repairs required by the utes, including replacements, differentials and gearboxes.

If we go back to the workplace and look at it in the context of operator ownership we find at many sites historically operator ownership of plant and equipment has often been forsaken for multi-skilling.

The Pendulum of Change – the History of Ownership within the Workplace

If we reflect back to the 1980s in Australia we find that many workplaces were highly demarcated, often with one person allocated to one machine or one area of responsibility. Although the operator was allocated to a machine or section of the plant, often they were supported by someone else who would clean the machine, someone else who would maintain the machine and in some cases someone else would set-up the machine or bring the raw materials to the machine, or remove the finished output. On the positive side, this did provide the opportunity to develop specialist skills and a level of ownership; however, the lack of flexibility often led to problems or frustrations when people are away or there is an urgent customer need requiring a quick response.

Since the late 1980s we saw the pendulum of change occur in our workplace with the introduction of multi-skilling to many sites. This involved the incentive (dash for cash) for the workforce to forgo many demarcations and take up new skills and responsibilities.

However, as some companies went through this experience, they noticed that quality and reliability problems started to increase.

Some realised that without a sense of 'ownership' personnel tend not to care for, or want to understand more, about their equipment or be in a place long enough to gain a very good understanding of their equipment.

> We still find today at some sites that enterprise agreements have been established over the past few years which require operators to move to different areas of the plant every 6 months so they can build up credits to move to the next pay level and receive a pay raise based on their overall plant flexibility. At these sites we also find management complaining that they are only getting average performance out of their plant and their operators!

Referring back to our example of the company ute versus the manager's car, both vehicles are the property of the company, yet the manager's vehicle, because of the perceived ownership of it by the manager, is often more reliable, performs better and has lower operating and servicing costs than the company ute which is driven by everyone and owned by no one.

This is because in a traditional multi-skilling environment our plant and equipment becomes like the company ute – performing poorly, often causing

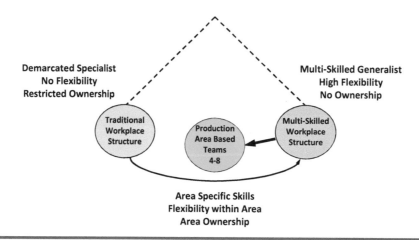

Figure 1.3 The pendulum of workplace change.

quality problems and has high operating and servicing costs which often lead to increases to the Maintenance Spend.

We are not saying multi-skilling was a bad idea. We believe in many cases we needed to move the pendulum across to get the change. Also, the experience of having our workforce go through a lot of retraining has been very positive. Multi-skilling has been successful in creating a more flexible workforce. However, experience now highlights that while personnel move from equipment to equipment, or area to area, they lose the motivation to seek out basic equipment problems or defects, which if left unchecked will cause failure in the future as shown previously. The operators often demonstrate a lack of understanding or care for the equipment because they know they will soon be moved to another area or piece of equipment (Figure 1.3).

Properly established Production Area Based Teams create an ownership environment that has flexibility though base skills across the team and promotes the development of mastery skills and team skills through on-going improvement activities.

Area Based Team Structure

Having recognised the limitations of the multi-skilling model, sites striving for Operational Excellence have moved to an Area Based Team model as shown in Figure 1.3. This is where teams are formed with a clearly defined area of responsibility and to ensure flexibility within the team every team member is trained in all the tasks required to achieve the production plan which we refer to as 'base skills.' Team members then go on to develop 'mastery skills' and 'team skills' so they can improve their area of responsibility.

The aim is to achieve the best of both worlds: ownership through defined areas of responsibility and flexibility through everyone in the team having the same 'base skills' to allow flexibility if anyone is temporarily away from the team, such as attending a Cross-functional Improvement Team meeting.

To understand more about what we mean by 'mastery skills' let us relate what we discovered from visiting a couple of sites.

Some years back we had the opportunity to visit one of Australia's largest wineries located in western Victoria. The winery was divided into two major sections: wine making and bottling. As you can imagine the wine making section was very seasonal in its activities, whereas the bottling hall operated 7 days a week all year long (grapes grow seasonally yet people tend to drink wine all year round).

We arrived on site quite early for a meeting with the bottling hall Maintenance Superintendent who was keen to introduce Total Production Maintenance (TPM) into the bottling hall. Unfortunately, the chap was in a bit of a flap because he had a 2-hour delay during the night shift on one of the main bottling lines and was trying to find out the details before the morning meeting with the Operations Manager. It appears the line stopped about 2.00 am and the Production Supervisor called the shift maintenance electrician, then moved the production crew off the line over to the cask line (other side of the bottling hall) while the electrician tried to get the bottling line going again. It appears the shift electrician started at one end of the line and systematically eliminated possible causes until finally at the other end of the line he found a proximity switch that had failed (or been broken). The problem had taken about 2 hours to find, and about 5 minutes to fix.

On hearing the story all we could do was sympathise with the Maintenance Superintendent as we had certainly had similar experiences in our maintenance days where the problem took forever to find yet once properly diagnosed it was quick to fix.

When we discuss this story in our public workshops we often find many people can relate to this situation.

About 6 months later we had the opportunity to visit the personal hygiene site at Wyong on the Central Coast – just north of Sydney in NSW, where they manufactured liquids such as shampoos, creams, body lotions and powders such as specialised laundry powders.

The Wyong site had been established some 5 years earlier following the closure and relocation of their old manufacturing facility in Sydney.

The site first tried TPM some 4 years earlier following a chap from the site completing a TPM Instructor's course in Japan. Unfortunately, the cultural shock of the Japanese push approach was too great and the initiative ceased after about 6 months. (It was trialled in the powders area and after 6 months all the operators refused to work with the chap because of the 'over-the-top' approach).

At the time, the OEE of the site was still only around 35% so it was decided to introduce a Process Reliability Strategy program based on an American project approach towards improvement. Initially they had some good successes and were able to raise the OEE to about 70%; however, they then stalled and couldn't seem to get any higher. Then they realised the limitations of a solely project approach to improvement. Hence after 2 years, they reintroduced TPM, however, this time using a more Australian sensitive methodology, which took a more behavioural approach engaging everyone across all shifts in TPM activities.

When we visited the site 2 years later, their OEE was consistently around the 85% mark for all their lines.

While visiting we saw a very impressive site. For example, a lot of the equipment's covers had been replaced with see-through plastic or Perspex with good lighting behind so that the operators could easily see any problems or equipment defects. Small tags were being used to highlight any equipment defects that were waiting to be rectified.

The TPM Manager was showing us around when we stopped at the back of the shampoo line's capping area to demonstrate how their equipment defect-tagging system worked. There was a tag on a hinge of one of the Perspex® panels. Unfortunately, when he grabbed hold of the tag to show it to us the hinge failed, and the panel came ajar from the machine activating a proximity switch which instantly stopped the line.

Suddenly, what appeared to be out of nowhere, a lady operator approached us asking 'what we had done to HER machine?' She very quickly re-adjusted the door and got the line going again. It was decided it might be best if we inspected other parts of the plant for a little while before coming back to the shampoo line.

When we did return the line was running perfectly and we were able to have a discussion with the operator about her TPM activities. While we were looking at all her impressive charts and sheets on the team Noticeboard, the line tripped out and stopped. The operator instantly excused herself and went over to the line, and progressively moved around the capping carousal systematically opening and checking each section. After about a minute, she found the problem, made some adjustments and had the line going again.

On her return to us, we asked the question: Did this problem happen often? Thinking this was a common problem and she had a standard task to rectify it. To our surprise, this was the first time something like this had happened and she was noting the event down for a discussion point and further investigation at her next TPM team meeting. My question to the manager was how did she know how to diagnose the problem so quickly? His answer was very quick and rather matter-of-fact as if the answer should be obvious to us. 'She has "mastery skills" for the capping part of the line'.

When we got back to the training room to review the site visit we asked the manager to expand on what he meant by 'mastery skills'. The visit to the winery some 6 months earlier came to mind, where the trained electrician took about

2 hours to find a problem, yet here on basically a similar bottling line (except the product tasted different) the operator had only taken about a minute. What were these mastery skills? Was this operator a trained tradesperson?

To explain his answer the manager drew four interconnect triangles on the whiteboard.

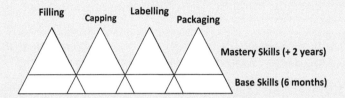

When they first set up the site, most of the operators were new employees so they instigated a policy of moving the operators around every 6 months to different areas of the plant. This way they felt they would have maximum flexibility within their workforce. However, as they progressed along the TPM journey for the second time, and hit the 70% OEE barrier, they realised this strategy was not ideal.

They discovered that it took the operators about 6 months to learn how to operate the equipment (base skill) to a good standard, but they were not able to develop any skills regarding understanding how the equipment functions (i.e. what is the role of a proximity switch and how does it work). Yet it was this 'mastery skill' of knowing how equipment functioned, how to diagnose problems and identify areas of weakness that would lead to best practice equipment performance which they had observed at TPM sites overseas.

This did not mean turning the operators into tradespeople. The operator we observed was not a tradesperson. She and her other three team mates had decided to divide the line into the four areas of filling, capping, labelling and packaging. They all picked an area and with the help of their allocated maintenance colleagues progressively learnt about how their area of the line functioned. They could all still, and did, help each other out by being very competent at operating and doing the changeovers on any part of the line. However, during their regular TPM improvement activities, each operator concentrated on their part of the line because they all agreed it would be too difficult to try to learn how the whole line functioned in the first instance.

Hence our learning has been that Area Based Team structure must support an ownership environment that has base skills and flexibility across the team and promotes the development of mastery skills and team skills through on-going improvement activities.

The next question we had was: How many people should we have in an Area Based Team?

Our experience and research indicated that 4 to 8 is the ideal size, which should include a designated working Frontline Leader (wages role rather than a salary role).

The '4 minimum' allows for flexibility. If the number is too small when one member of the team is temporally away, say attending a Cross-functional Improvement Team meeting, it can put a strain on the other team members to cover for them.

The '8' is an interesting number. We often hear numbers like 10 or 12 for the maximum.

The reason we have selected 8 is to do with understanding the true purpose of an Area Based Team. We believe the true purpose is to create synergy within a group of personnel so that their output as a team will be much greater than they could achieve individually.

Some people describe synergy as $1+1=3$.

A good Australian sporting example of synergy would be the doubles tennis players known as the 'Woodies' (Todd Woodbridge and Mark Woodforde).

The Woodies combined Woodforde's left-handed baseline play with Woodbridge's swift volleying reflexes at the net. They were the ATP Doubles Team of the Year four times and won 61 ATP doubles tournaments as a pair.

The Woodies won eleven Grand Slam doubles titles in their career – one French Open, two Australian Opens, two U.S. Opens, and a record six Wimbledon wins.

Their other career highlights included winning a gold medal at the 1996 Atlanta Olympics, and a silver medal at the 2000 Sydney Olympics.

The Woodies often teamed together to play for Australia in the Davis Cup, and played for Australia in three Davis Cup finals. They helped give Australia its first Davis Cup victory in 13 years in 1999 with a win over France's Olivier Delaitre and Fabrice Santoro in Paris.

The pairing ended in 2000 after Mark Woodforde retired from international tennis.

Individually they were not rated very highly on the singles circuit, however, in a doubles game, even against the top two seeded singles players, they would always win because they played by knowing and supporting each other's weaknesses and they played to each other's strengths, hence producing a greater result than neither could do individually.

Another sporting example would be the 'Oarsome Foursome' which was a famous Australian rowing team.

The **Oarsome Foursome** is the nickname for an Australian rowing crew who competed between 1990 and 1998 winning two Olympic gold medals in the coxless fours.

The original crew was Nick Green, James Tomkins, Mike McKay and Sam Patten. Patten was replaced by Andrew Cooper in 1991–92 and by Drew Ginn from 1995.

They won:

Olympic gold: 1992, 1996

World Championship gold: 1990, 1991, 1998. (coxed four)

Individually they won very few medals; however, together they won two Olympic gold medals and three World Championship gold medals as a team.

The key to synergy is good team chemistry. We have found that the larger the team the harder it is to generate good team chemistry. You can do it with teams larger than eight, however, our experience has shown it takes a lot more effort and support. We find, as the teams get bigger members tend to form inner clans within the team. This can lead to factions within the team that inevitably produces poor team chemistry and, hence, inability to create the team synergy within the team, necessary for that greater level of performance.

Another good reason for keeping the team size to eight is that, as per Rule 4 from the paper 'Decoding the DNA of the Toyota Production System' by Steven Spear and H. Kent Bowen, we want all leaders to be teachers. Toyota found it very difficult for anyone to competently teach more than seven in a workplace environment so, hence, seven team members and a Frontline Leader make a team of eight. They also found that a span of control of greater than seven gets too large to properly manage where the development of people is a key focus.

In an Operations Excellence environment, apart from understanding and following the site's required induction or core skills covering policies and procedures for working at the site, Area Based Team should have 4–8 members including a designated working Frontline Leader and they require:	
Base Skills	Able to operate all equipment/work stations within the team's area of responsibility
Mastery Skills	Understand functioning of equipment and be able to diagnose at the earliest possible time equipment and quality problems at the source for their allocated piece or pieces of equipment within their team's area of responsibility
Team Skills	Able to be an effective team member and positively contribute to their team as it progresses through the 4 Stages of Area Based Team Development

The 4 Stages of Area Based Team Development

We first came across this concept at Tennessee Eastman Company in America back in the late 1980s after their first attempt at TPM failed. They thought TPM was about creating self-empowered Production Area Based Teams who would take responsibility for their work and hence, they wouldn't need as many supervisors. They also thought TPM was about transferring tasks between operators and maintainers. In other words, they were looking for quick cost savings.

TPM is about reducing costs; unfortunately, it is a lot subtler than Tennessee Eastman realised.

After about 12 months of removing a lot of their supervisors, they came to realise that the teams were incapable of working as a synergistic team and managing their own workplaces. They then, after much research, developed what we call the Four Phases of Production Area Based Team Development model. They found there are four distinct phases to production team development and that they had to train their production teams and allow them time to develop before moving them through each phase. Their experience was that on average it took a team about 9 months to gain enough experience to move through to the next phase. In other words, to go from 'undeveloped' to 'mature' took about 3 years.

This experience at Tennessee Eastman is certainly not dissimilar to what we have seen during the 1990s in many Australasian companies where they have rushed into creating self-directed production teams by giving everyone training, say over a weekend, then expecting the teams to perform.

Effective or synergistic production teams do not happen naturally, then need to develop. As such we have found the Tennessee Eastman four phases to developing a mature synergistic Production Area Based Team a very helpful model to follow.

When we first establish Production Area Based Team improvement activities, many team members are not sure of how to work as a team.

1. Undeveloped	At this stage we have found we need to be very prescriptive in providing clear direction or guidelines on how to go about improvement activities.
2. Experimenting	At this stage teams are more open to trying new things however they still need clear direction or guidance on what needs to be done.
3. Consolidating	At this stage the team is demonstrating their capability at knowing what needs to be done
4. Mature	At this stage we should have a synergistic team that knows what needs to be done to achieve the required outcomes

In Australasia, due to our upbringing, the majority of us are very good individuals, but lack the experience of working effectively within a team.

This is where the difference between Japan and Australasia is very important to understand.

In Japan, children are often taught how to work in a team environment from their days in kindergarten or pre-school. For example, at kindergarten the activity for the children might be to paint a picture of a house. In a typical Australian kindergarten each child will be placed in front of their easel and expected to produce a painting, which can be taken home for parents to admire and maybe pin up or display. Hence, they produce their own individual picture. Whereas in a typical Japanese kindergarten, the children are often placed in teams of three or four and together they paint a house with one doing the walls, another the roof, another the garden, etc., and the picture is displayed at the kindergarten for all the parents to come and see and admire their child's work they did with their team.

In Australia, our education system tends to bring students up as individuals. When doing exams at school and university, even if students wanted to work with their fellow students as a team they would be told to do their exams by themselves!

Another example of team development is watching kids play team sports for the first time. Down from our office there is a soccer field where they have the junior league. Have you ever seen little 6- or 7-year-olds play soccer for the first season? They all have the basic individual skills of being able to run and kick a ball; however, when you put them into a team all they want to do is run and kick the ball irrespective what their team mates are doing. Often the poor coach is on the field trying to keep them separated so they don't accidentally kick each other.

After the experience of a season, and the players have developed an understanding of space and positions, the coach can stay off the field and just run up and down the sideline fending off the parents on one side and directing the kids on the other side!

More seasons later on, the coach does not have to run up and down the sideline as the kids are more experienced at what to do, and finally in senior grades during the game the coach just approaches the team at half time.

This is the same for the workplace. Many people have very good individual skills to do tasks; however, when you first put them in a team they tend to upset other people by not considering their contribution. This is why the role of the Frontline Leader and Level 1 Salary person (e.g. supervisor) is so critical.

Tennessee Eastman found that their supervisors (Level 1 Salary) had to go through similar stages of development as the Area Based Teams did.

In a lot of companies, supervisors are very good at ensuring their Area Based Teams produce the required output; however, they do not have a lot of experience in engaging and developing their frontline leaders and their team members especially, in improvement activities. In other words, they spend most of their time on ensuring tasks are getting done, with little time left to devote to developing their people and improving processes.

For this transition to successfully occur, we find that supervisors need good leadership support and experienced facilitation guidance to assist their learning. In some cases, a supervisor may not wish to make this transition, in which case we suggest they become part of the technical support group for the Area Based Teams.

Tennessee Eastman also found that when the teams were 'undeveloped' you needed a supervisor for each team. By the time the teams reach the 'mature' stage (after about 3 years) they only needed one supervisor per 3–7 teams supported by properly developed frontline leaders. The redundant supervisors either voluntarily retired or became part of the technical support group.

Hence, if there is not an awareness of this transitional process, and the time and expert guidance provided for it, there is a risk the whole process will fail (rejection by the supervisors who feel uncomfortable and threatened by the new way). Without the skills and support, people will become anxious and hence resist the change.

We have found in Australasia it can typically take a team about 6–12 months per phase or some 3 years for it to progress through the four phases of Area Based Team development. The Frontline Leader supported by their supervisor also needs to progress through the same phases.

Another key learning has been that the best way to develop teams is to use a 'boundary management' approach. This entails setting clear boundaries for the teams and reviewing and expanding the boundaries as the teams move into each phase of their development. The purpose of the boundaries is to protect both the teams and the company.

To more fully explain what we mean by boundary management let us use 'learning to drive a car' as an example.

When a young person reaches driving age, do we just throw them the keys to the V-8 and say 'go to it kid' or do we have a process for them to follow to become a competent driver?

As a responsible society, we use boundaries to assist them to develop their driving skills.

First, they are required to be of a certain age, and then they are required to pass a competency test to verify that they know the road rules. We then give them their Learner Licence and place boundaries on them including that they must have a licensed person sitting next to them when they drive. They have speed restrictions and drug and alcohol restrictions. They are also required to keep a log book to verify their driving experience.

Once they go for their next license what happens to the boundaries? They are not totally lifted but rather expanded. They don't need a licensed driver with them; however, they need to display a red P plate and they still have speed restrictions (80 k/h) and drug and alcohol restrictions.

After 12 months, if they have a good record, the boundaries are expanded again; however, some still exist (in NSW a green P plate which lifts the speed restriction from 80 k/h to 100 k/h).

What is the purpose of the boundaries – who are they designed to protect?

They are designed to protect both the driver and the public.

Boundary management for Area Based Teams is very similar. They are designed to protect both the team and the company.

Examples of team boundaries used during improvement activities would be:

Type	Scope
Physical:	What area the team is responsible to improve?
Technology:	Can we make changes to technology during our activities or is the improvement restricted to existing technology?
Team Resources:	How much time can we allocate to our activities?
Support Resources:	How much time can maintenance allocate to support our team?
Financial:	How much money have we got to spend, and how do we justify if we need more?
Meetings:	When can we have our meetings?
Changes:	What do we have to do before we can change something?

Further Learning from Area Based Team Structure

Earlier we discussed Area Based Team structure and identified that the ideal size of a team was 4–8, which included a working Frontline Leader. We would like to expand on this important learning by further examining why there is a need to limit the number of direct reports to any leader at a site to 7.

We have created a simple model that helps explain the concept of having no more the 7 people directly reporting to a person.

It is based on Rule 4 from the paper 'Decoding the DNA of the Toyota Production System' referred to earlier, which states 'Any improvement must be made in accordance with the scientific method, under the guidance of a teacher, at the lowest possible level in the organisation'. This infers that all leaders are to be teachers of problem solving. We, similar to Toyota, have found that if you want your leaders to be teachers they should only have a maximum of 7 people directly reporting to them (Figure 1.4).

Initially, you may think this is an extremely inefficient way to structure an organisation, creating far too many layers. When we look at the model presented and do the sums relating to reporting numbers, it is actually a very efficient way to structure an organisation.

If we have Production Area Based Teams with designated frontline leaders (wages role) of 4–8 reporting to a Level 1 Salary person such as a supervisor, and the supervisor has 3–7 frontline leaders as direct reports, the total number of people reporting to the supervisor would range from 3 teams of 4 people which equates to 12 people, or in the maximum situation 7 teams of 8 people which equates to 56 people.

If we have 3–7 Level 1 Salary persons or supervisors reporting to a Level 2 Salary person such as a manager, the total number of people reporting to the manager would range from 39 people if there were 3 supervisors each with 3

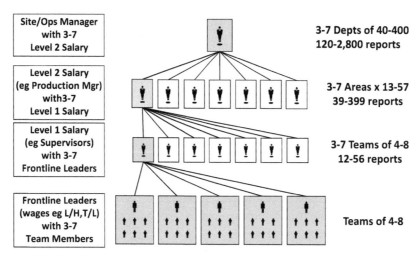

Note: At small sites one or two levels could be eliminated

Figure 1.4 **Structure that supports the development of your people.**

frontline leaders with 3 team members, or 399 people if there were 7 supervisors each with 7 frontline leaders with 7 team members.

If we have 3–7 Level 2 Salary persons or managers reporting to the Site Manager or Operations Manager, the total number of people reporting to the Site Manager or Operations Manager would range from 120 people if there were 3 managers each with 3 supervisors with 3 frontline leaders with 3 team members, or 2,800 people if there were 7 managers each with 7 supervisors with 7 front-line leaders with 7 team members.

As you can see, this structure can have up to 400 with just two staff levels: the supervisors reporting to the manager. By adding the extra level, you have the capacity to increase the total site to 2,800, yet no one has any more than 7 direct reports.

How does this framework compare to your site?

In some cases, it can be very similar; however, at some sites we come across we find some Level 1 Salary (e.g. supervisors) have 12–20 direct reports based on the traditional thinking that a supervisors main role is to ensure the correct tasks are completed by their direct reports.

Also, at a lot of sites we come across the Frontline Leader level is often a technical Leading Hand role or Senior Operator role where all they do is provide technical solutions when asked, rather than leading and developing the Area Based Team to ensure it achieves the Production or Work Plan in a safe, quality, cost-effective and environmentally sound way each shift.

One site we worked with in Tasmania many years ago had a packing hall structure of some 25 people running a number of lines and reporting to the supervisor level with no effective frontline leaders. Multi-skilling was a high priority, so people were regularly moved to different lines to ensure flexibility.

We strongly recommended they select and train suitable existing operators into the Frontline Leader role so as to create a 4–8 structure. Many excuses were given for over 18 months before they finally took the action. Amazingly for them (not to us) the OEE of their packing lines increased by 20% within 3 months of settling in their new frontline leaders and Area Based Team structure with ownership to agreed lines, without increasing the overall number or people within the packing area.

Another key aspect of ownership and accountability in the workplace is the arrangements with key support staff to production such as maintenance, quality, etc. Too often we find support staff on conflicting roster systems to production such that there is no direct alignment to allow regular contact and relationships to be developed to promote open sharing of information and learning. This is particularly critical relating to maintenance support.

At sites where operators interact with plant and equipment through adjustments, changeovers, replenishing of packaging materials, etc., Operational Excellence should include the application of TPM thinking where operators learn to care for their plant and equipment and identify problems and issues with the plant and equipment at the earliest possible time to allow the Maintenance department to rectify small, inexpensive problems before they become significant problems. For TPM to be effective, all the production areas need to have a dedicated maintenance person to support the TPM activities and develop mastery skills about their allocated area. This doesn't mean the maintenance person only works in their dedicated area, as they need to be flexible and assist in all other areas as required; however, for a dedicated period of time each week they should be allocated to support the TPM activities, and ideally be the allocated maintenance person to attend the relevant Daily Review Meetings.

This, therefore, requires production and maintenance rosters to be aligned or supportive such that maintenance can catch up with their Production Area Based Team or Teams on a regular basis.

Ideally, if Production Area Based Teams are on 12-hour rosters you would want the Maintenance department to be on the same 12-hour roster pattern or be available on regular dayshift. Being on regular dayshift is what we mean by supportive.

In the finishing department at a lead smelter, they had production on a 12-hour 2x dayshift, 2x nightshift, 4 days off roster involving 4 crews. The area maintenance support person was on 5 day 8-hour dayshift roster. This way all shifts knew when the maintenance person was available and, on most occasions, he was available to each crew during their second dayshift when they would do their TPM training and activities.

> When crews are working 12-hour x 2x dayshift, 2x nightshift rosters we recommend improvement activity be conducted in the morning of the second dayshift. We find after having 4 days off, most crews need the first dayshift to get orientated, so by doing the improvement activity on the morning of the second dayshift they still have the afternoon of the dayshift and their 2 nightshifts to complete or follow-up on anything.

We often come across sites where production and maintenance rosters are not aligned or supportive. The reason for the misalignment can often be put down to previous management's focus of finding the cheapest short-term way of getting access to equipment for the maintenance people rather than developing the skills of their operators to find equipment problems at the earliest possible time.

The sites that try to proceed with TPM without aligning their production and maintenance rosters typically find the development of the operators is compromised.

It is a bit like a child going off to primary school where the relationship with the teacher is very critical for the child to embrace learning. For example, if they get on well with the teacher they often progress well, whereas if they don't get on well or don't like their teacher, they often lose interest and lag behind.

Changing maintenance support all the time is a bit like your child getting a different teacher all the time. Communication will often be constrained by both parties, hence slowing up the learning process.

We have also found that not only maintenance, but also quality and mentoring support must comply with Rule 2 from the paper 'Decoding the DNA of the Toyota Production System' referred to earlier:

'Every customer-supplier connection must be direct, and there must be an unambiguous yes-or-no way to send requests and receive responses'.

When Production Area Based Teams commence their TPM improvement activities it is critical this is all worked out and documented for the team before kicking off the activities. We use a tool called a Team Information Sheet to ensure this happens. This is a sheet completed before a team commences its improvement activities. It documents the Team's mandate, boundaries, leader, members and designated support people covering mechanical and electrical maintenance, quality, safety, mentor and facilitator.

The Need to Address All Failures, Not Just Equipment Failures

We started off talking about equipment failures with the main cause being lack of understanding or desire to care.

If we think further about this concept, it should also be applied to all failures whether they are safety, quality, delivery, inventory or any other of the sites Key Success Factors for Operations referred to in Figure 3.1 in Chapter 3.

Hence, creating ownership through Area Based Teams to unleash the full potential of your people by developing base skills, mastery skills and team skills is the foundation to addressing any of your problems at the source.

However, we need to recognise the critical importance doing this in a framework of the 4 Stages of Team Development supported by boundary management along with an aligned and effective support structure covering maintenance, quality, safety and environment, management mentoring and good facilitation.

Effective daily management requires a supportive structure that promotes both the development of people and ownership within the workplace so there will be accountability for performance and responsibility for support. From a production perspective, this is best achieved with Production Area Based Teams, each with a properly trained Frontline Leader (typically a wages person spending less than 50% of their time operating the plant), and no more than 7 direct reports (operators). Each Production Area Based Team should have a clear 'Area of Responsibility' for achieving the production plan in a safe, quality, cost-effective and environmentally sound way.

The frontline leaders should report to a Level 1 Salary person, where all Level 1 Salary persons should have no more than 7 direct reports so that they, like the frontline leaders, can be responsible for the training and development of their direct reports.

To implement such a structure, the site should be divided into production areas where performance can be measured (e.g. input and good output can be measured), such as standalone production lines like a bottling line or packaging line.

Each production area, or group of production areas if they are small, should have a Production Area Based Team responsible for each shift.

If the production area is large and requires more than 7 operators to run it, then it should be divided into 'Areas of Responsibility' such as front-end and back-end with a Production Area Based Team (designated Frontline Leader and up to 7 direct reports) responsible for each 'Area of Responsibility'.

Without ownership by both production and maintenance to clearly defined production areas through correct structure and accountability, Daily Review Meetings tend to be data gathering exercises supported by general discussions rather than effective meetings focused on ensuring issues affecting performance are properly addressed and supported.

Chapter 2

Effective Frontline Leaders – Element 2

What Do We Mean by Frontline Leader?

In the traditional or Mass Production days – before the concepts of Lean Production were exposed in the book *The Machine that Change the World,* by Womack, Jones and Roos in 1990 – we had leading hands or line specialists who tended to be the best operator in the area that others would go to for assistance. They were typically responsible for ensuring the set-ups or changeovers were done properly and spent most of their other time operating the plant or showing new operators how to operate the plant. In recognition, they were paid more than an operator and were often given first preference for overtime.

To support the leading hands, there would be a supervisor or Level 1 Salary person who would be responsible for achieving the production plan in a cost-effective way while also being responsible for ensuring that everyone under their control complied with all company policies. Typically, they would spend as much time as possible on the shop floor ensuring everyone was busy and the lines were running.

Regarding improvement, this was left to the industrial engineers, process specialists or project engineers with the shop floor expecting to do what they were told. Hence, many workers took the attitude of 'leave my brain at the gate because all the company wants are my hands and feet'.

The New Approach

The Frontline Leader should play a pivotal role in both reactive and pro-active improvement while management should ensure a Stable Production or Work Plan through flow logic. This will create an environment where the Frontline Leader can focus without the disruption of the fire-fighting associated with unexpected production or work plan changes (refer to Figure I.1: The three critical parts of a continuous improvement strategy).

Since 2004, Professor Jeffrey K. Liker from the Industrial and Operations faculty at the University of Michigan in the U.S., has been a very successful prolific writer of books explaining the Toyota Way. One of his book's was published in 2007 and titled *Toyota Talent: Developing your People the Toyota Way*. In Chapter 2: 'Toyota Works Hard to Develop Exceptional People', Liker explains how the Toyota Production System's chief architect Taiichi Ohno, as he implemented single-piece flow, soon learnt it would not work by relying on the traditional model of industrial engineers telling the workforce what to do.

'A select few front-office experts could not possibly deal with all the situations that would surely arise. He needed capable masses. The development of capable masses requires a clear plan. It requires time and patience. Above all, it takes persistence and the willingness to stick with it and to deal with the individual peculiarities and challenges of each person' (Liker, 2007).

The above confirms the view that we need to develop our frontline people if we are to be successful. Without effective Frontline Leaders to support the development of the frontline people it won't happen.

Further developments in the thinking regarding the role of a Frontline Leader can be found in the book *Leadership – Making Lean a Success* first published in Sweden in 2013. One of the key messages we found in the book was the concept of Management by Means of standardised work as opposed to the more traditional approach of management by results (Figure 2.1).

This reinforces the importance for Frontline Leaders to be allowed sufficient time to train, monitor and support their crew in order to carry out their tasks to the agreed standards rather than just getting things done.

Like Toyota, by really understanding the principles behind 'Lean Thinking' you can then determine the best way to move forward. At Toyota they

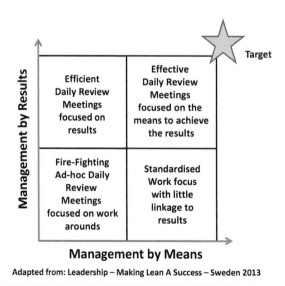

Adapted from: Leadership – Making Lean A Success – Sweden 2013

Figure 2.1   Management by means versus management by results.

recognised the need to develop their frontline people (e.g. operators) so that they can find problems at the earliest possible time by:

- **Establishing standards** so that frontline people could immediately identify if something was not to 'standard' e.g. identify problems.
- **Practicing zero defects accepted,** meaning if it is not to the required standard, reject it (put in the red bin) or if necessary 'pull the cord' and stop the line so that problems can be immediately addressed.
- **Developing Frontline Leaders** who could demonstrate and teach how to operate the plant to the required standard and how to identify problems (deviations to standard) at the earliest possible time.

Based on the above, a Frontline Leader that can support Operational Excellence is typically a wages person with a group or team of workers, e.g. operators, reporting to them. Titles can vary such as leading hands, team leaders, section leaders, etc.; however, the title Frontline Leader does infer a leadership element to the role.

It is a working role that takes on a number of the responsibilities traditionally done by Level 1 Salary personnel (e.g. supervisors).

As they are not salary employees, they normally do not have the authority to discipline their direct reports, however their main focus should be to teach and develop their direct reports so as to create a safer, more productive and harmonious workplace. Another way of expressing this could be to say, their role is to create synergy within their work group or team so their output and achievements are far greater than what a group of individual workers could achieve.

As a working role they would also be required to cover for their direct reports when they are off the line during part of their shift due to training or Cross-functional Improvement Team activities, for example. As such there should be clear guidelines or rules governing how much time can be allocated to working the line as opposed to leading and developing their crew. Ideally, they should be spending no more than 20–40% of their time operating/setting up the plant during a normal day.

What Should Be the Allocation of Time for a Frontline Leader Supporting Operational Excellence?

Below is an example, however, your goal will be influenced by the nature of the work being carried out by the Frontline Leader and their crew (direct reports) and the number of direct reports involved (Table 2.1).

If the Frontline Leader is required to spend too much time working the line, the Level 1 Salary person they report to will find themselves 'working down a level' and doing some of the duties or tasks that the Frontline leader should be doing while leaving gaps in doing their Level 1 Salary role which will need to be filled by their Level 2 Salary person they report to, and so on. In other words, if the Frontline Leader is not effective because they are spending too much time

Table 2.1 **Example Allocation of Time for a Production Frontline Leader**

Activity/Focus	Example	Current	Your Goal
Ensure tasks are completed by their crew so that the Production Plan is achieved in a safe, quality and cost-effective way	50%		
Develop the skills of their crew through competency based training	20%		
Lead or support On-going Improvement activities	10%		
Operate the Line or Plant to cover short-term absences during the shift	20%		

working the line, *everyone else in the leadership structure tend to work down a level* and productivity and morale of the work group will significantly decline.

What Structure and Rosters Should We Have to Support the Development of Our Frontline Leaders?

Professor Jeffrey L. Liker, in his book *The Toyota Way – 14 Management Principles of the World's Greatest Manufacturer* published in 2004, outlined the structure that had been developed by Toyota. It was based on the principle that no leader should have any more than seven direct reports so that they are able to teach all their direct reports problem solving, visual workplace and Prevention at Source, which underpins the Toyota Production System.

This thinking was also raised by Steven Spear and H. Kent Bowen in their paper 'Decoding the DNA of the Toyota Production System', published in the *Harvard Business Review* in September/October 1999, where their 4th rule covering how to improve stipulates that 'any improvement to production activities, to connections between workers or machines, or to pathways must be made in accordance with the scientific method, under the guidance of a teacher and at the lowest possible organisational level'. In other words, the Frontline Leader needs to be a teacher of problem solving to their team members (direct reports) and their supervisor (Level 1 Salary person) needs to be the teacher of problem solving to them. Meanwhile the manager (Level 2 Salary person) should be the teacher of problem solving to the supervisor (Level 1 Salary person) (Figure 2.2).

If the aim is to develop your Frontline Leaders so they are able to teach and develop their direct reports, we have found, like Toyota during the 1960s, as they developed their Toyota Production System, that they should have no more than seven direct reports. We often refer to Area Based Teams consisting of 4–8 people including a designated Frontline Leader. The limit of eight is based on a number of learnings:

■ Teams of greater than eight often form small sub groups which can be detrimental for creating synergy within the team;

No Leader has any more than 7 direct reports

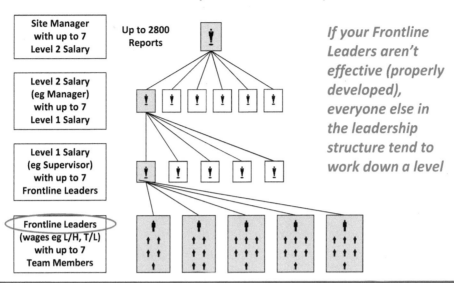

If your Frontline Leaders aren't effective (properly developed), everyone else in the leadership structure tend to work down a level

Figure 2.2 Example structure that supports the development of Frontline Leaders.

■ If you want your team to develop total flexibility where each team member is able to do all the tasks or operate all the work stations within the team's area of responsibility you may be constrained by the complexity of learning (too many work stations to learn) for each team member; and

■ The larger the crew size the harder it is for the Frontline Leader to train and develop, especially if there are new members or new technologies being introduced.

If the Frontline Leader has more than seven people reporting to them, then we suggest you consider splitting the production area into Areas of Responsibility with 4–8 people including a Frontline Leader in each of these areas. This is to ensure your Frontline Leaders can focus on the development of their team members rather than just focus on allocating and monitoring tasks to a large group of more than seven people.

Another key aspect we have found is the relationship between the Frontline Leader and support people, such as maintenance and quality, is crucial as the Frontline Leader will be relying on support people to help them learn about caring for the equipment and finding equipment and quality problems at the earliest possible time so they can develop their crew. As such, production rosters and support staff rosters (e.g. maintenance) should be aligned or supportive to build relationships and promote the sharing of learning.

Another issue we have found at some sites is where the Frontline Leaders report to more than one Level 1 Salary person. The logic given is to allow better communication between shifts; however, what we have found is that the Frontline Leaders tend to take advantage of the situation by playing one Level 1 Salary person against another so they always get their way – a bit like children who first ask mum for permission to do something and if they don't get the answer they want, they will go to dad before mum has updated dad on the situation, and ask it in a slightly different way so they get the answer they want. Then when mum finds out that dad has agreed when she said no, there can be conflict between mum and dad.

As such, the communication issue between shifts should be addressed with a better hand-over process and the use of continuous improvement (CI) tools such as improvement sheets where all shifts sign-off on improvements before any crew implements them, and all Frontline Leaders should only report to one Level 1 Salary person so they can properly coach, train and develop their crew.

What Should Be the Roles and Responsibilities of a Frontline Leader?

Before developing competent and engaged Frontline Leaders, we need to determine and document what the Frontline Leader's roles and responsibilities should be, so they understand where they fit into the organisational structure and the level of leadership they will assume. Most of what we expect from our Frontline Leaders can be covered by the following areas of focus:

0. Understand and Reinforce Company Policies and Procedures
1. Safety and Environment
2. Quality
3. Achieve the Production or Work Plan
4. Reactive Improvement/Daily Management
5. Pro-active Improvement
6. Work Area Management/5 S
7. Equipment Management
8. Energy/Resource Management

Possible Key Roles

■ Ensure company policies and procedures are followed and adhered to;
■ Ensure required tasks of the team are completed to standard;
■ Ensure the achievement of the Production Plan or Work Plan in a safe, quality, cost-effective and environmentally sound way;
■ Train and support team members in base skills (ability to do all required tasks within their area of responsibility);
■ Train and support team members in team skills (ability to be a contributing team member);
■ Teach team members to be successful in Frontline Problem-Solving Root Cause Analysis;
■ Teach team members to be successful in creating a visual workplace so that any deviations from standard can be identified at the earliest possible time; and
■ Teach team members to be successful at Prevention at Source through zero defects accepted, clean for inspection, train for inspection and manage by inspection so as to stop problems from occurring (Table 2.2).

Table 2.2 Possible Areas of Focus and Key Responsibilities of a Frontline Leader

Areas of Focus	Key Responsibilities
0. Policies & Procedures	• Ensure everyone is ready to start on time; • Ensure all have the required Personal Protective Equipment (PPE) and are wearing such; • Conduct 10 min start of shift meeting to reflect on issues from previous 24 hours and ensure everyone understands the expectations for the coming shift/24 hours; • Ensure breaks are taken at the correct time; • Ensure everyone returns from breaks at correct time; • Ensure area of responsibility (workplace) is left to the agreed standard at end of shift; • Ensure everyone concludes the shift at the correct time; and • Ensure there is a proper hand-over to the next shift.
1. Safety & Environment	• Ensure safety and environment policies and procedures are adhered to at all times; • Conduct risk assessments; • Rapidly rectify any workplace hazards; • Rapidly initiate accident investigation following any accident within workplace; • Rapidly initiate incident investigation following any incident (damage to property or environment) within workplace; and • Rapidly initiate hazard control (minimise, isolate, eliminate).
2. Quality	• Ensure all team members understand the quality standards for all inputs and practice 'zero defects accepted'; • Ensure all team members understand the quality standards for all outputs and practice 'zero defects passed on'; • Ensure all team members understand the thinking behind statistical process control and variation so that all adjustments are appropriate and recorded; • Rapidly respond to any input defects identified by the team members (check all red bins at least every hour); • Confirm routine quality checks and address any issues; and • Rapidly respond to out-of-control conditions and/or quality problems.
3. Achieve the Production or Work Plan	• Process start-up and control; • Meet production goals; • Respond to production problems raised by team members; • Cover temporary absenteeism (no longer than 2 hours per shift); • Ensure parts/materials are supplied to process; • Report/track hourly production results; • Identify the training needs of team members; • Plan and deliver on-the-job training to team members to enhance their base skills; • Update training and assessment records of team members; and • Ensure issues and learning are communicated effectively to the Frontline Leaders on other shifts.

(Continued)

Table 2.2 (Continued)   Possible Areas of Focus and Key Responsibilities of a Frontline Leader

Areas of Focus	Key Responsibilities
4. Reactive Improvement/ Daily Management	• Conduct Start of Shift Review Meeting with all direct reports to reflect on previous 24 hours performance, initiate Frontline Problem-Solving Root Cause Analysis when appropriate, confirm requirements for the shift and set priorities for the team, ensure everyone understand expectations for the coming shift/24 hours; • Attend daily Level 1 Salary Meeting to report the performance of their area of responsibility, update on the progress of team goals and escalate any issues outside the boundaries of their team; and • Support all team members as they participate and contribute in Frontline Problem-Solving Root Cause Analysis activities, e.g. Cause & Effect and 5 Why Analysis (Root Cause Analysis).
5. Pro-active Improvement	• Be a member of, or lead, a Cross-functional Improvement Team; • Lead Area Based Team improvement activities such as Work Area Management/5 S; • Support all team members as they participate as a member of a Cross-functional Improvement Team; • Support team members as they identify and act on small improvement initiatives; • Plan and prioritise small improvement initiatives and allocate tasks; • Lead team through self-assessments of their Area Based Team improvement activities and address any shortfalls; and • Lead team through team skills self-assessment each cycle.
6. Work Area Management/5S	• Raise work orders for approved improvements; • Ensure all agreed work area standards are adhered to; • Ensure the wastes of 'unnecessary movement' and 'transportation or conveyance' are minimised or eliminated; and • Co-ordinate priority of improvements with maintenance support.
7. Equipment Management	• Raise work orders for urgent maintenance support; • Confirm and support weekly Maintenance Plan; • Co-ordinate operator equipment management activities with Maintenance Plan activities; and • Co-ordinate priority of equipment defect list with maintenance support.
8. Energy/ Resource Management	• Confirm routine energy/resource management checks and address any issues; and • Rapidly respond to out-of-control energy/resource management conditions and/or problems.

The above is a guide only as each site, and in many cases each production area, may have specific requirements.

It should also be noted that once you create your roles and responsibilities document it will be very unlikely that your existing Frontline Leaders will be immediately capable of fulfilling everything listed. This should not be seen as a deterrent but rather an opportunity to grow your Frontline Leaders using the roles and responsibilities document to map out a development plan for them that ideally will be linked to your Continuous Improvement/Operational Excellence road map or master plan.

Coaching of Team Members

To assist the development of the Frontline Leader and reinforce their teaching of base skills, the Frontline Leader and their Level 1 Salary person they report to, should be coaching the team members on a daily basis while they are completing their tasks by asking such questions as:

- How do you know what is coming to you is correct?
- How do you do this work?
- How do you know you are doing this work correctly?
- How do you know that the outcome is to the required quality standard (free of defects)?
- What do you do if you have a problem?

This regular process of asking specific questions in a positive and encouraging way gives the team member increasingly deeper insights into his or her own specific work while also highlighting to the Frontline Leader and their Level 1 Salary person any deficiencies in their training methods.

What Attributes Should We Develop in Our Frontline Leaders?

Operational Excellence comes from taking the long-term view, patiently developing people and leaders and treating all personnel as appreciating assets, rather than just focusing on checklists and tools.

Professor Jeffrey K. Liker and Gary L. Convis cover this topic in their book *The Toyota Way to Lean Leadership* published in 2011, where they identify some of the key attributes of a Frontline Leader as:

- A commitment to excellence;
- A willingness and desire to learn a new way of thinking;
- A willingness and desire to learn a new way of leading;
- See their role as one of developing their people and creating future leaders, in other words, a desire to be a good teacher and long-term thinker;
- Recognise that safety first is a given, and that perfect quality and customer satisfaction are the most important focus of the company after safety; and
- Understand and reinforce that safety and quality are never sacrificed for cost or expediency.

If the above attributes are desired of your Frontline Leaders, then the challenge becomes who should teach and reinforce these attributes. Obviously, it should be the role of the Level 1 Salary person (e.g. supervisor) they report to.

Then who should teach and reinforce these attributes to the Level 1 Salary personnel? Obviously, the Level 2 Salary person (e.g. manager) they report to.

The message we are trying to give is that the Management Team needs to determine the attributes they would like their Frontline Leaders to have to support their journey to Operational Excellence, then teach and reinforce these attributes throughout all levels of leadership within the site.

The key is to create an environment in the workplace where the attributes can be discussed and reinforced on at least a daily basis.

Creating the desired behaviour of Frontline Leaders can be influenced either by the environment they are placed in or the attitudes they have. We have found working on the environment is a much easier and quicker way to get a change in behaviour recognising changing attitudes can take some time.

As such the role of the Management Team is to create an environment where the Frontline Leader is encouraged to behave with the desired attributes. In other words what situation can we place the Frontline Leader in each day where the desired attributes are demonstrated and reinforced? (Figure 2.3).

One method to teach, demonstrate and reinforce the desired attributes is for the Level 1 Salary person (e.g. supervisor) to do regular coaching of their Frontline Leaders, while they are coaching their team members as outlined previously in Coaching of Team Members.

Another method to teach, demonstrate and reinforce the desired attributes is to use the Daily Review Meeting process which should be part of the focus of your reactive improvement activities which will be covered in detail in Chapter 4.

What Skills Should We Develop in Our Frontline Leaders?

During the Second World War, the concept of Training within Industry (TWI) was developed in the U.S. (1940) to accelerate the training of new or unskilled employees in factories who replaced those who joined the military and went

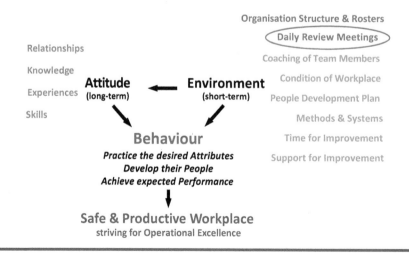

Figure 2.3 Creating the desired behaviour.

off to war. Without the TWI methodology, which kept the factories producing at maximum output, the war effort would have been severely impacted. The focus was on how to produce products safely, quickly, correctly and conscientiously.

The TWI methodology was the foundation used by Toyota after the war to address their training needs as they developed and cascaded their Toyota Production System throughout Toyota sites around the world.

In the paper 'The Roots of Lean, Training Within Industry: The Origin of Japanese Management and Kaizen', Jim Huntzinger describes the five needs of a Production Leader:

1. Knowledge of the Work (equipment, products, skills to make the products)
2. Knowledge of Responsibility (policies, agreements, schedules)
3. Skill in Instructing (job instruction)
4. Skill in Improving Methods (job methods)
5. Skill in Leading (job relations)

We have taken these needs and created six frameworks for the skills development of Production Frontline Leaders to support the development of effective Work Groups or Area Based Teams (hence the addition of team work skills):

1. Knowledge of Responsibilities (policies and procedures)
2. Knowledge of Work (basic skills)
3. Skill in Instructing (teaching skills)
4. Skill in Improving (mastery skills)
5. Skill in Team Work (team skills)
6. Skill in Leading (leadership skills)

Below are examples of some of the things you may wish to consider under each framework.

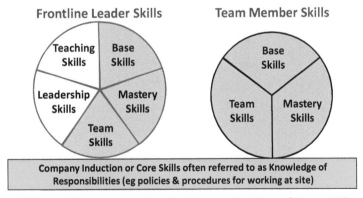

Frontline Leader Skills

Teaching Skills | Base Skills
Leadership Skills | Mastery Skills
Team Skills

Team Member Skills

Base Skills
Team Skills | Mastery Skills

Company Induction or Core Skills often referred to as Knowledge of Responsibilities (eg policies & procedures for working at site)

Base Skills: Able to operate all work stations in their Area of Responsibility to agreed standards

Mastery Skills: Problem Solving, Visual Workplace, Prevention at Source

Figure 2.4   **Skills required for effective Area Based Teams.**

1. Knowledge of Responsibilities (Policies and Procedures)

- Ensure all policies and procedures are up-to-date and easily accessible, then ensure the Frontline Leader is properly trained in them, and demonstrate their competency through testing and observing/coaching by supervisor;
- Develop effective Level 1 Salary (e.g. supervisor) Daily Review Meeting where several Frontline Leaders report on the entire performance of their Area of Responsibility; and
- Ensure Level 1 Salary person (e.g. supervisor) coaches their Frontline Leaders to conduct effective start of shift meetings.

2. Knowledge of Work (Base Skills)

Review the current base skills status of the Frontline Leader and their crew (team members) by reviewing the current Base Skills Matrix, provided it exists and is up-to-date. It should highlight that:

- Everyone has the ability to competently operate all the plant and equipment within their team's area of responsibility;
- All team members have sufficient skills flexibility to allow all operators to cover for each other in the various tasks required to achieve the production plan and, hence, be able to rotate around the various tasks on a regular basis so there is total ownership of their Area of Responsibility; and
- Everyone can cover their fellow team members while they are involved in training and on-going continuous improvement activities to develop their mastery skills.

If a current Base Skills Matrix does not exist or is questionable, rather than trying to update the Base Skills Matrix, which can sometimes cause concern by the workforce, we suggest an Education & Training Operator Base Skills Team is established to:

- Verify centreline settings;
- Identify any equipment weaknesses that could impact on holding the centreline settings;
- Confirm standards for inputs and outputs;
- Ensure standard operating procedures based on the TWI format[1] and supported by job instructions are up-to-date, easy to understand and explain why each key step is required; and
- Ensure there is an objective competency assessment process supported by an appropriately designed Base Skills Matrix.

Refer to the Centre for TPM booklet: *Understanding the Concepts of Training within Industry and Standardised Work*, available at: www.ctpm.org.au Then assist the frontline leader to train all their crew to their required competency level, and then create a new up-to-date Base Skills Matrix to confirm who has been properly trained and to what level.

3. Skill in Instructing (Teaching Skills)

A key instructing skill for a Frontline Leader is their awareness of their team member's individual learning styles along with their current abilities and interests. As such formal training in 'Knowing your Learners' can be very helpful. This should also be supplemented with formal training in the various training methods to identify the most effective methods for their team members.

4. Skill in Improving (Mastery Skills)

- Member of Cross-functional Improvement Team;
- Lead a Cross-functional Improvement Team;
- Always be a member or lead a Cross-functional Improvement Team; and
- Lead Area Based Team improvement activities (5 S/Work Area Management and the four stages involving the 7 Steps of Autonomous Maintenance/ Operator Equipment Management).

5. Skill in Team Work (Team Skills)

We have identified 10 team skills that Frontline Leaders should be aware of and be able to train their team members in. An effective way of developing these skills is to have your Frontline Leaders initially go through the training with other Frontline Leaders, then support their team as they go through the training often in modules of up to 2 hours with relevant practical activities included (Table 2.3).

6. Skill in Leading (Leadership Skills)

We have identified three foundational leadership skills for Frontline Leaders which can be presented in modules of up to 2 hours with other Frontline Leaders (Table 2.4).

Team Skills, Teaching Skills and Leadership Skills Training

Team Skills

Before having the Frontline Leader's Team go through a Team Skills module we strongly recommend that the Frontline Leader be given the typical 2-hour Team Skills training modules with other Frontline Leaders so as to develop a good understanding before their teams are given the team skills training.

Priority of the training can be established by having the Frontline Leaders and their Level 1 Salary person they report to reflect on their teams by completing a Team Skills Assessment before finalising the order of the training program. Alternatively, if your Frontline Leaders and their teams are involved in Area Based Team Pro-active Improvement activities such as 5 S/Work Area Management or

Table 2.3 **Team Skills Modules Objectives and Content**

Team Skill Module	Objective	Content
# 1 **Team Effectiveness**	To build each team member's knowledge, giving them a better understanding of what a team is, the motivations of their colleagues and how their contributions can excel or hinder their team's performance. Throughout this training session, the team will discuss their ideas and complete a number of activities. This aims to give them a greater knowledge of what their strengths and weaknesses are as a team, and what needs to be done in order to become a more 'Effective Team'.	• What a team is? • Why we need team work? • Forming an effective Area Based Team • Stages of team development • How your team measures up? • Characteristics of a good team member
# 2 **Effective Area Based Team Meetings**	To give teams a better understanding of how effective their team meeting skills are at the present, through the use of an 'Effective Meeting Rating Sheet'. Then provide them with helpful information and hints so that they can improve their practices for future meetings	• The importance of meetings • What can go wrong? • Responsibilities of team members • Requirements for effective meetings (preparation, organising, meeting, participation, keeping order, ending the meeting)
# 3 **Presentation Skills**	To give teams a better understanding of the power presentations can have when communicating an important message to others. Through the use of handy tips, exercises and steps to follow, this training session aims to develop each team member's presentation skills and give them a new-found confidence and enthusiasm when it comes to presenting.	• Why we give presentations? • Planning for a presentation • Structure of a presentation • Using visual aids • General tips • Importance of practicing • Improving your presentations • The top 10 ways to feel confident about public speaking
# 4 **Decision Making and Problem Solving**	To give teams a range of skills and techniques to help them solve problems and make decisions as a team rather than as individuals. If decisions are made together, everyone in the team will be a lot more willing to participate resulting in a more successful collaborative result.	• Decision making and problem-solving overview • Paired Comparison Analysis • Grid Analysis • Plus/Minus/Interesting (PMI) • Star-bursting

(Continued)

Table 2.3 (Continued)   **Team Skills Modules Objectives and Content**

Team Skill Module	*Objective*	*Content*
# 5 **Dealing with Difficult People**	To educate teams on overcoming difficulties they may arise due to other team member's behaviour and attitudes. This training session shows that all teams, even the best, run into problems because of 'difficult people'. During the session, an understanding of why people are difficult will be developed and steps to overcome these difficulties will be learnt and put to use.	• Who are difficult people? • Potential reasons for difficulties • The DON'TS of dealing with difficult people • Skills and strategies to resolve issues • Empathy • Case Study: William Jones • Helpful tips to deal with difficult people
# 6 **Conflict Resolution**	To foster teamwork and improve relationships by managing conflict within teams and the workplace as a whole. This training session shows the importance of addressing conflict in its earlier stages and provides the teams with a plan of action and handy hints to help them resolve the conflicts that may arise at any time.	• What is conflict? • Common problems with teams • Conflict development • Thomas-Kilmann Conflict Strategy (Self-Assessment) • Thomas-Kilmann Conflict Model • Resolving conflict • Handy hints – when resolving conflict • Benefits of conflict
# 7 **Negotiation Techniques**	To emphasise the importance of using good negotiation techniques when it comes to gaining agreement about a decision or when solving a problem that has arisen. Good negotiation techniques can keep a relationship in good steeds and make both people or parties feel like they have come out on top. During the training session, the team/s will be introduced to a 'Negotiation Model', which will take them step by step through the negotiation process. The team/s will also be introduced to the key skills that should constantly be considered and developed.	• Negotiation • Negotiation styles • Negotiation models • Key skills • Obstacles in negotiation

(Continued)

Table 2.3 (Continued) **Team Skills Modules Objectives and Content**

Team Skill Module	Objective	Content
# 8 Appreciation of Individual Strengths and Weaknesses	To give each team member a better understanding of the different behavioural styles that may be present within their team and workplace as a whole.	• Individual behavioural styles • Identifying your behavioural style • Individual strengths and weaknesses • Adapting behaviours to become better team members • Taking action
	Within this training session the teams will learn all about the different behavioural styles that exist, think about their own behavioural styles and develop the knowledge of how to handle each behavioural style they may come across within their workplace or team. Each behavioural style has strengths and weaknesses, if they are dealt with in the correct manner, you can get the best out of any person.	
# 9 Giving and Receiving Feedback	To explain the importance of on-going feedback within a team and within a workplace. Through the use of positive and negative feedback (if done in the correct manner), workers and team mates can develop and improve their skills. During the training session the team/s will be introduced to the concept of feedback and will be taken through the most successful way of both giving and receiving feedback, because we feel that they are equally important.	• Feedback • Harmful feedback • Giving constructive feedback • Receiving feedback • Try writing it – Written feedback • Why use feedback?
# 10 Planning and Prioritising	To train team members to prioritise their tasks and to not get distracted by unimportant time wasters. In doing this teams will achieve more in shorter amounts of time, resulting in better results and less stress. Within the training session planning and prioritising tips and techniques will be given and activities will be undertaken to test the newly learnt knowledge.	• Planning • How to plan? • Identifying time robbers • What is prioritising? • Priority groups • How to prioritise? • Reward yourself

Table 2.4 Leadership Modules Objectives and Content for Frontline Leaders

Leadership Module	Objective	Content
# 1 **Time Management and Delegating**	To reflect on how you really spend your work time and what can be done to get the most out of your time.	• Goal setting • Prioritisation • Managing interruptions • Procrastination • Scheduling • Know how you spend your time • Delegation process • Work Time Management Action Plan
# 2 **Motivation and Accountability**	Motivate your team members to complete tasks to required standards (standardised work). Motivate your team members to become fully engaged in on-going continuous improvement.	• Team member motivation • Intrinsic motivation • Extrinsic motivation • Achievement motivation • Loss of motivation • Accountability • Care and Growth Model • Do incentives work?
# 3 **Evaluating Leadership (Self Development)**	Provide a framework for self evaluation.	• Evaluating your leadership/training • Leadership self evaluation

Autonomous Maintenance/Operator Equipment Management then each team member could evaluate their current team skills using the same Team Skills Assessment with the feedback used to prioritise which modules would be given first ensuring a good buy-in from the team members for the training.

Team Skills Assessment

Assess each of the 10 Team Skills by ticking the appropriate box for each of the 4 statements relating to each Team Skill to indicate your team's performance throughout their last Improvement Cycle or past 12 weeks.

It is important to answer as truthfully as you can, so that your team can identify its strengths and discover any weaknesses that can be developed through further training and experience.

Scoring is based on: **Often = 5; Sometimes = 3; Rarely = 1.** The lowest Total Score out of 20 indicates the biggest opportunity for improving Team Skills.

1. Effective Team Members:	Often	Sometimes	Rarely	Score
Workload is shared throughout the team with each member taking charge of their own role				
Team members communicate and collaborate (work together) to achieve their outcomes				
Team members constantly look for ways to better use materials, processes and resources. Sharing their findings with their team				

Team members are committed to and are accountable for a common purpose and performance goal				
			TOTAL:	/20
2. Running Effective Meetings:	**Often**	**Sometimes**	**Rarely**	**Score**
Clear objectives and a purpose it set prior to the meetings. Appropriate tools, agendas, task sheets are used throughout				
Meetings focus on achieving consensus				
Team maintains adequate level of discipline and punctuality. Leaving personal conversations at the door				
Meetings end with summaries of all decisions so that each team member is aware of their roles and assigned tasks				
			TOTAL:	/20
3. Presentation Skills:	**Often**	**Sometimes**	**Rarely**	**Score**
Each team member knows the subject and purpose of the presentation they are giving				
Presentations follow a logical sequence (Introduction, content and summary) making sure adequate time is allocated				
Relevant and appropriate visual aids are used to enhance the presentation				
Effective communication skills are demonstrated during presentations (loud and clear voice, eye contact, harness non-verbal communication and active listening)				
			TOTAL:	/20
4. Decision Making and Problem Solving:	**Often**	**Sometimes**	**Rarely**	**Score**
Decisions are made based on facts and data rather than on gut feel or experience				
Problem-solving tools and techniques are used properly and effectively to ensure we address the root cause(s) of our problems				
Agreement from all other shifts in your Defined Production Area (DPA) is obtained before implementing solutions				
Decision making involves all team members and is based on consensus				
			TOTAL:	/20

5. Dealing with Difficult People:	Often	Sometimes	Rarely	Score
Team members understand the diversity of their team and their behaviours				
When difficulties arise within a team, decisions are made promptly on what course of action that will be taken (time, location and who is involved)				
Team members react in a positive way to problems and suggestions				
Team members show understanding and empathy while emphasising the need to change				
			TOTAL:	/20
6. Conflict Resolution:	Often	Sometimes	Rarely	Score
Conflicts are managed appropriately within the team, understanding that conflict only becomes destructive when it degrades human dignity				
Conflicts are addressed as soon as possible so that the team can move forward				
Team members listen effectively to each other and ask questions to help them understand the issues that arise				
Negotiation techniques are used to help solve conflict with the team				
			TOTAL:	/20
7. Negotiation Techniques:	Often	Sometimes	Rarely	Score
A negotiation process is used within the team to resolve differences so as to reach mutual agreement				
Team members practice the communication skills of listening, questioning and creatively looking for alternative solutions				
The objectives are always kept in mind as well as the wishes of the people involved				
Team members are aware of the obstacles that may inhibit reaching mutual agreement				
			TOTAL:	/20
8. Appreciation of Individual Strengths and Weaknesses:	Often	Sometimes	Rarely	Score
Team members are aware of their own and other team member's behaviour patterns and personalities				

Team members are aware of their own and other members weaknesses and strengths				
Roles and responsibilities are assigned based on an individual's strengths/capacities/abilities				
Strategies are developed as a team to overcome any weaknesses that may affect teamwork				
			TOTAL:	**/20**
9. Giving and Receiving Feedback:	**Often**	**Sometimes**	**Rarely**	**Score**
Feedback is given on a regular basis in a respectful and supportive manner				
When feedback is given, it is clear, specific and emphasises on the positive				
Team members recognise the value of the feedback and listen without interruption or objections				
All feedback given is used by the team to grow and develop				
			TOTAL:	**/20**
10. Planning and Prioritising:	**Often**	**Sometimes**	**Rarely**	**Score**
Team activities are planned on a regular basis				
Plans that are created include setting objectives, deciding on how to achieve those objectives and implementation of the plan				
All team members recognise the difference between the important, the urgent and the unnecessary				
Team members are realistic when planning and allocating jobs ('you cannot do everything in one day')				
			TOTAL:	**/20**

Teaching Skills and Leadership Skills

Once the team skills modules have been successfully completed, or if more appropriate, in parallel while progressing the team skills modules (e.g. develop a plan that best suits your needs), we suggest the Frontline Leaders complete the 2-hour teaching skills and leadership skills training modules with other Frontline Leaders so as to develop teaching and team leadership competencies.

We suggest a formal Frontline Leader development program be established covering the 15 modules above with a module being delivered either weekly of fortnightly to allow the Frontline Leaders to practice their learning in their workplace supported by their Level 1 Salary person daily coaching. (It is assumed that the Level 1 Salary person of the Frontline Leaders has successfully completed similar training and can coach their Frontline Leaders daily to reinforce their learning – if this is not the situation, we suggest the Level 1 Salary person does the training with the Frontline Leaders.)

What Should Be a Typical Day/Week of a Frontline Leader?

Below is a list of possible tasks for a Frontline Leader during a typical or standard day or shift to **ensure Tasks are completed by their crew so that the Production Plan is achieved in a safe, quality and cost-effective way (refer Table 2.1)**:

- Conduct hand-over meeting with previous shift (if appropriate);
- Prepare for start of shift e.g. confirm production plan, raw materials availability, equipment ready;
- Prepare for Start of Shift Meeting;
- Conduct Start of Shift Meeting with all of their crew;
- Conduct standard start-up procedure (if appropriate);
- Conduct hourly monitoring of line performance including reviewing scrap, rework or 'red bins', raw material status etc.;
- Prepare for supervisor Daily Review Meeting e.g. product samples, performance data etc.;
- Attend supervisor Daily Review Meeting;
- Respond to actions generated at Start of Shift and Daily Review Meetings;
- Conduct end of shift workplace standards inspection; and
- Conduct end of shift hand-over.

Below is a list of possible extra tasks for a Frontline Leader during a typical or standard week required to Lead or support On-going Improvement activities (refer Table 2.1):

- Attend their Cross-functional Improvement Team meeting;
- Prepare for or conduct activity to support their Cross-functional Improvement Team;
- Lead their Area Based Team improvement weekly meeting; and
- Lead their Area Based Team improvement weekly activities.

Once the standard work plan is established for a Frontline Leader, ensure all other leaders and support staff respect the plan by not calling meetings or scheduling other activities involving the Frontline Leader that will conflict with the agreed plan.

If the Frontline Leader is required to leave their workplace then arrangements should be put in place such as the Level 1 Salary person (e.g. supervisor) they report to or their second in charge (someone in their team they are developing to be a future Frontline Leader), to ensure the Frontline Leader standard work is completed e.g. hourly monitoring of line performance including review 'red bins', raw material status etc.

As the Frontline Leader develops, the initial standard work plan may expand, we suggest you review the amount of time allocated to the activities at least every 3–4 months and adjust accordingly.

What Is the Best Way to Develop the Desired Attributes and Skills of Our Frontline Leaders?

1. Ensure your structure will support the Frontline Leader role;
2. Determine and document the roles and responsibilities of the Frontline Leader for each area then assess each Frontline Leader to determine any gaps that need to be addressed – establish a plan to address the gaps;
3. Determine and document the attributes you would like to develop in your Frontline Leaders;
4. Develop and implement a Daily Review Meeting plan that will support the development of your Frontline Leaders;
5. Review all company/site policies and procedures to ensure they are up-to-date and easily accessible then retrain/refresh all Frontline Leaders to the required site competency standard;
6. Introduce Frontline Leader standard work;
7. Review all operator base skills in area and supporting quality standards, standard operating procedures, and if deficient establish an education and training operator base skills team to address such;
8. Train Frontline Leader in **instructing skills**;
9. Ensure the Frontline Leader is a member of, or leads, a Cross-functional Improvement Team every cycle;
10. If an Education and Training Operator Base Skills Team has been established have the Frontline Leader train their crew in the new base skills to the required competency level;
11. Train Frontline Leaders in **team skills**; and
12. Train Frontline Leaders in **leadership skills**.

Use of Skills Matrices

As Frontline Leaders and their team members (Area Based Team) develop, their progress should be captured using appropriate skills matrices. We suggest the following skills matrices should be developed for each Area Based Team:

- Knowledge of Responsibilities Skills Matrix;
- Base Skills Matrix;
- Mastery Skills Matrix;
- Team Skills Matrix;

And for Frontline Leaders:

■ Teaching Skills Matrix; and
■ Leadership Skills Matrix.

Summary Checklist for Developing Frontline Leaders

Any approach needs to be tailored to suit the specific situation; however, this summary checklist highlights the issues and their possible impact.

#	Issues Often Found	Yes	No	If Not Addressed	Suggested Action if Yes
1	Production Frontline Leaders span of control greater than seven people			Production Frontline Leaders don't have the time to properly and regularly train and develop their direct reports	**Structure and Rosters** Align rosters and establish Production Area Based Teams of 4–8 members including a designated Frontline Leader
2	Production and maintenance rosters not aligned or supportive			The same maintainers can't support the Frontline Leader and their crew to build a trusting relationship where information is shared freely	
3	No current roles and responsibilities document exists for Frontline Leaders			Frontline Leaders and the people they report to are unclear as to the roles and responsibilities of the Frontline Leader	**Roles and Responsibilities** Determine and document the roles and responsibilities of the Frontline Leader
4	No current attributes document exists for Frontline Leaders			Possibility of inconsistent behaviours of Frontline Leaders	**Attributes** Determine and document the attributes you wish to develop in your Frontline Leaders
5	No coordinated site Daily Review Meeting Plan exists			May result in support staff not being regularly available for Daily Review Meetings	**Daily Management** Initiate *Reactive Improvement* to improve daily management practices and processes
6	Ineffective Level 1 (e.g. supervisor) daily management processes (e.g. ineffective Daily Review Meetings, information centres and problem-solving capability)			Significantly reduce opportunity to develop Frontline Leaders, and may result in a lot of fire-fighting and work-arounds limiting time for Frontline Leaders to be effective	

#	Issues Often Found	Yes	No	If Not Addressed	Suggested Action if Yes
7	Poorly trained and ineffective Frontline Leaders			Level 1 Salary person (e.g. supervisors) and Level 2 Salary person (e.g. manager) need to work down a level to compensate	**Standards and Base Skills** Initiate *Education and Training Operator Base Skills* Cross-functional Teams to set the operational standards and develop base skills of all Frontline Leaders and operators in all shift crews
8	Poor or no standards across shifts resulting in variation in operations			Make it a lot harder to identify the root cause(s) of problems	
9	Production Area Based Teams of 4–8 lack flexibility in that all members can't cover for everyone in their team			Difficult to develop improvement areas with strong ownership by operators to allow effective Area Based Team improvement activities	
10	There is no leader standard work for the Frontline Leaders			Inconsistent performance of Frontline Leaders resulting in variation in Production Area Based Team performance	**Frontline Leader Standard Work** Initiate the development of Frontline Leader standard work and apply across all Frontline Leaders with support from all support departments

Note

1. Refer to the Centre for TPM booklet: *Understanding the Concepts of Training within Industry and Standardised Work*, available at: www.ctpm.org.au

Chapter 3

Appropriate Measures – Element 3: Key Success Factors for Operations

A key foundation for Operational Excellence is to have goal-aligned performance measures. This is where all measures at all levels of the operation are aligned to the Key Success Factors for Operations. In other words, all measures should be based on, and reported under, your site's Key Success Factors for Operations so that everyone can see where their performance contributes to the overall site performance.

Before we look at what measures should be reported on at each level we need to understand the Key Success Factors for Operations (Figure 3.1).

We can divide key success factors into *causal* and *effect*. In other words what causes us to have an effect?

In the case of operations, it is all about achieving a required cost or financial performance so that the business achieves its required Return on Investment. Without the required Return on Investment the operation will more than likely lose its ability to source further investment and there will be a push to reduce spending on long-term essentials, such as people development and preventive maintenance, all of which sends a site down the spiral of decline.

Hence the 'effect' is cost/financial performance. The 'Causal' Key Success Factors are the things that cause us to either make or lose money from an operational perspective, and most importantly most can be measured and reported on a weekly, daily, by shift and even hourly basis, whereas most financial measures are reported monthly and hence provide a 'rear view mirror' perspective of performance.

'Cause' Key Success Factors

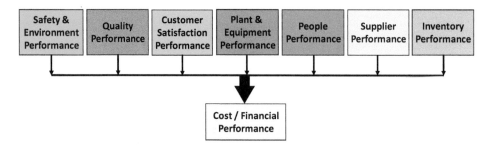

Figure 3.1   Example Key Success Factor for Operations model.

In the table below we have listed the most common Causal Key Success Factors which we come across in a typical manufacturing or mining company and the possible impact if they are not right.

Causal Key Success Factor	Effect If Not Right
Safety and Environment Performance	If we have accidents, injuries or incidents it can be very disruptive and cost a lot of money
Quality Performance	If we don't get things right the first time, we will waste a lot of materials and time resulting in higher costs
Customer Satisfaction Performance	If we don't satisfy our internal and external customers with delivery and quality expectations we will cause delays in our processes, lose sales or have a lot of claims resulting in loss of income
Plant and Equipment Performance	If our plant and equipment does not perform well and is not looked after we will lose capacity and have higher maintenance costs
People Performance	If people don't turn up or are not productive, or don't find problems at the earliest possible time we will end up with higher costs
Supplier Performance	If our suppliers let us down or provide inferior goods or services, our costs will go up
Inventory Performance	If we carry too much inventory, we will have too much cash tied up in the business which can incur interest costs, or if we don't have enough inventory we can miss opportunities or delay operations

Some companies like to:

■ Use different names such as Human Resource Performance rather than People Performance;

- Split the Causal Key Success Factors into more headings; or
- Reduce the number.

However, from our experience if you can keep it to eight or less headings including cost/financial performance it makes it easier to create scoreboards. The less complicated the better, as it allows your people to have a clearer 'line of sight' or better alignment to company goals.

This is important because the aim of goal alignment is to allow anyone in the business to see how their input is affecting the site performance. For example, the safety performance in one area will feed into the safety performance of the entire site.

Order Is Important

When establishing the Causal Key Success Factors we find the order is very important because even if we tell everyone they are all important, people, especially your managers or leaders, will prioritise their actions around their perceived order of importance. For example, the Quality Manager may perceive quality is more important than delivery and will advise the despatch area to hold off on delivering an order to a customer until further quality checks are carried out, whereas the Production Manager may perceive delivering on time and meeting delivery targets is more important and instruct the Despatch Department to send the order because it must be there by an agreed time or before month end to allow invoicing. Meanwhile, your workforce in despatch become confused, and more than likely, would not make decisions themselves because they know if they did they will displease one of the management team.

We should never forget the maxim: *'Measures dictate Behaviour'*.

The initial order we have used is safety first then quality, which is influenced by the book: *The Toyota Way to Lean Leadership* by Jeffrey K. Liker and Gary L. Convis, where they state, 'quality is never sacrificed for cost or expediency'. The remaining order can vary from site to site, so we are using the most common order we come across, recognising that at your site you may have different priorities and hence use a different order.

For example, at some sites we come across the operation is very dependent on manual assembly of the products with little machinery to assist apart from a sealer at the end. In these situations, you often find the People Performance Key Success Factor is moved in front of the Plant and Equipment Performance Key Success Factor.

We see it as the role of the Site Management Team (Site Manager and direct reports) to determine on a consensus basis, the order of the Key Success Factors they want for the site so that all scoreboards covering site, department, area and crew are created based on the appropriate Key Success Factors as the headings in the agreed order.

Establishing Performance Measures

Once the Key Success Factors are agreed, you can then group your performance measures under the appropriate heading. This way you immediately see if there are any gaps in what you are currently measuring.

At one site, the Management Team selected what they thought were the appropriate measures and placed them under their Key Success Factor headings. Each week they highlighted with a large green tick or a red cross whether they achieved target or not. During a visit we noticed that all the performance measures under the Causal Key Success Factors were a green tick yet the Effect Key Success Factor of cost/financial performance was a red cross. This didn't make sense as the logic is 'if all the casual measures are on target, then the effect should be on target'. When challenged, the Management Team realised they were not measuring a critical raw material inventory issue that had blown out over the past 2 weeks having a significant impact on costs.

Ideally, we have found that 2–3 performance measures per Key Success Factor should be sufficient so as not to make the scoreboard too complex or difficult to quickly comprehend.

Some helpful rules to apply when establishing the measures are:

■ Have all charts set up to report weekly with 26 weeks displayed allowing targets to be reviewed and changed every 6 months;
■ Have all charts set up so that trends up are good and trends down are not good;
■ Have all scoreboards standardised so that the same measures are located in the same place on all scoreboards;
■ Ensure the site scoreboard sets the minimum standard for all other scoreboards regarding layout, accuracy, clarity and timeliness; and
■ Ensure all key areas of measurement for operations are covered on the scoreboard.

Displaying Your Performance Measures

The next action should be to agree on how the measures should be displayed so there is a site standard created that is easy to tell the status and trend as you walk past say 2 metres from the scoreboard. Typically, sites will start with a site scoreboard that has all 'causal' measures reported on a weekly basis using printed coloured bar charts, where a green bar indicates that the target or expectation has been achieved or exceeded and a red bar indicates that the target has been missed. On the other hand, we have found at Daily Review

Meetings where performance is measured daily, and daily run charts are created for the month to monitor trends. A simple hand drawn run chart is preferred over a bar chart as we don't want people wasting their time colouring in bar charts each day.

How to create the site scoreboard is also an issue. Some want to go for very fancy solid boards which are fixed to the wall and each chart is printed on the board. Our experience suggests a simpler pilot approach is often a better way to start. As such, we tracked down tri-fold display boards (www.foamboards.com.au), which can be very quickly and cheaply established to test out the layout and choice of measures before going to a more permanent solution. The foamboards also proved to be very helpful being displayed in the workplace where everyone walks past, yet easily collected and carried to the meeting room for all to see when doing the weekly review meeting (Figures 3.2 through 3.4).

Once the design of the site scoreboards is finalised, the next step is to populate the scoreboards so it can be easily seen how performance is tracking, and place them in an area with high foot traffic (where most people walk at the site) (Figure 3.5 and Figure 3.6).

Establishing a Baseline and Targets

If you don't know where you are, how can you get to where you want to be?

When embarking on your improvement journey you should establish a starting point or baseline, and then quantify your improvement vision.

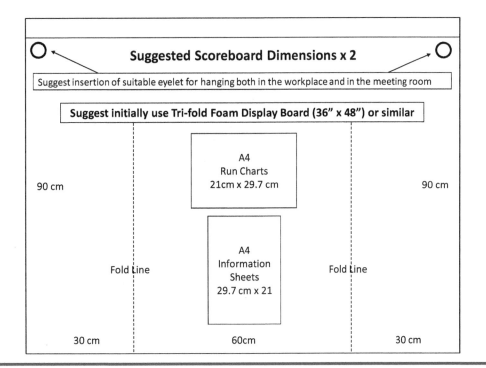

Figure 3.2 Suggested initial scoreboard material and dimensions.

Sample Site Scoreboard 1			
Safety, Health & Environment	**Quality**	**Customer Satisfaction**	**Plant & Equipment**
Zero Harm, Zero Incidents	Do it right First Time; eliminate all Waste	Delivery in Full, on Time, within Spec	Perfect Equipment Performance & Reliability
Safety All Injuries Weekly Chart	**% Scrap** Weekly Chart	**Delivery** Weekly Chart	**Unplanned Downtime** Weekly Chart of Site
Environment Incidents Weekly Chart	**% Yield Loss** Weekly Chart of Site	**Customer Complaints** Weekly Chart	**OEE** (A x R x Q) Weekly Chart of Bottleneck Line
Summary Baseline & Targets	**% Rework** Weekly Chart	**Output** Weekly Chart	**% PM Compliance** Weekly Chart

Figure 3.3   Sample site scoreboard layouts.

Sample Site Scoreboard 2			
People	**Supplier**	**Inventory**	**Costs**
Effective People engaged in the Business	Reliable, High Quality Suppliers	Appropriate Inventory Levels	Most Cost Effective Producer
Productivity Weekly Chart	**Supplier Delivery** Weekly Chart	**RM Stock Levels** Weekly Chart	**Energy Cost / Output** Weekly Chart
Unplanned Absences Weekly Chart	**Supplier Quality** Weekly Chart	**WIP Stock Levels** Weekly Chart	**Maint Cost / Output** Weekly Chart
Continuous Improvement Time Weekly Chart		**FG Stock Levels** Weekly Chart	**Total Cost / Output** Weekly Chart

Figure 3.4   Sample site scoreboard layouts.

For example, if your improvement vision is to achieve Operational Excellence as outlined in Figure I.1 and your timeframe is 5 years, then you should be able to quantify what you expect your performance to be in 5 years using the Key Success Factors for Operations model developed in Figure 3.1.

Figure 3.5   **Example locations of site scoreboards.**

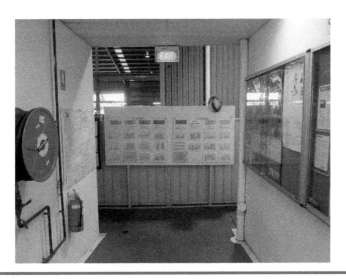

Figure 3.6   **Example locations of site scoreboards.**

A useful process for doing this is outlined below:

1. Establish the Key Success Factors for Operations along with relevant performance measures and definitions
2. Determine timeframes for determining the baseline and the annual results to allow monitoring of progress – timeframe for comparing performance is normally the previous 6 week average if it is a weekly measure, and previous 3-month average if it is a monthly measure; all measures should be reviewed weekly apart from the costs or financials as they are normally locked into monthly reporting
3. Baseline current performance to allow monitoring of progress
4. Establish your target timeframe for achieving world class performance – our experience in most cases is a 5-year timeframe as the most realistic target

5. Establish targets for world class performance – targets are normally determined using one of four methods depending on the measure:

   a. Absolutes such as zero for accidents or 100% for delivery;
   b. Calculated based on agreed assumptions as in the situation for Overall Equipment Effectiveness (OEE)[1];
   c. Benchmark to compare reported best practice from another site or company to set your target; or
   d. Upper control limit – where you create a run chart of the performance and use statistical process control equations to determine the upper control limit, which you then make as your target.

6. Establish annual targets to support world class targets – targets are normally determined using three methods depending on what you are measuring and the expected impact from improvement:

   a. Linear where improvement will have a consistent impact over the next 5 years;
   b. Upward exponential where you expect most of the improvement to occur in the later part of the 5 years after all the foundation work has been completed; and
   c. Downward exponential where you expect a lot of gains from the 'low hanging fruit' in the early years with improvement becoming harder in the later years. (Figure 3.7)

Key Success Factors	Performance Measures	Definitions	Baseline (date)	Year 1 Target	Year 2 Target	Year 3 Target	Year 4 Target	Year 5 Target
Safety & Environment	Injury Freq Rate	Per million man hrs	18	15	12	9	5	0
	Incident Freq Rate	Per million man hrs	100	80	60	40	20	0
	Environmental Incidents	# Incidents per 12 months	5	4	3	2	1	0
Quality	Scrap	% Total Processed	20%	15%	11%	8%	4%	1%
	Rework	% Hrs / Avail Hrs	8%	6%	4%	2%	1%	0%
	Yield	% Recovery	90%	91%	92%	94%	96%	98%
Customer Satisfaction	Delivery to Customer	% DIFOTQ	98%	98%	99%	100%	100%	100%
	Customer Complaints (Ext)	Complaints – ppm	50	40	30	20	10	0
	Achievement of Prod Plan	% Achieved	89%	92%	94%	96%	98%	100%
	Lead Time (top Value Stream)	Days or Hours	5 days	4 days	3 days	2 days	1 day	4 hrs
Plant & Equipment	Unplanned Downtime	% Available Time	20%	15%	10%	5%	3%	2%
	OEE (bottleneck line)	HLOEE Equation	60%	70%	75%	80%	85%	87%
	Capacity	Output / Week	160kt	185kt	200kt	210kt	225kt	230kt
People	Productivity	Good Output / worked hrs	20	23	26	30	35	40
	Unplanned Absenteeism	% Hrs worked	6%	4%	3%	2%	1%	1%
	On-going CI Time	% Hrs / Worked Hrs	1%	2%	4%	6%	8%	10%
Supplier	On Time Delivery	% Items Purchased	75%	80%	85%	90%	95%	99.9%
	Quality Issues	% Items Purchased	5%	4%	3%	2%	1%	0.1%
Inventory	Raw Materials Inventory	Days of Sales	14	13	11	9	7	5
	Work In Progress Inventory	Days of Sales	21	17	13	9	5	3
	Finished Goods Inventory	Days of Sales	14	12	10	8	5	3
Costs	Maint Cost	$ / output	$0.60	$0.55	$0.50	$0.45	$0.35	$0.30
	Prod Cost	$ / output	$2.40	$2.20	$2.00	$1.80	$1.60	$1.50
	Energy Cost	$ / output	$0.70	$0.68	$0.65	$0.60	$0.58	$0.55
	Total Cost / Output	$ / output	$9.50	$9.00	$8.00	$7.00	$6.50	$6.00
Timeframe for Comparing Performance is typically 6 week average if a weekly measure, and 3 month average if a monthly measure								

Figure 3.7   Sample site baseline measures and targets.

Call to Action

We recognise it can be quite daunting establishing a baseline that will capture all your performance outcomes across your entire operation; it is never easy. The important thing to remember is that in order to improve your current performance you need to establish a baseline so that you know exactly what impact your improvement activities are having.

'You Can't Manage What You Can't Measure'

The Site Management Team should have an initial go at confirming or establishing the site's Key Success Factors for Operations, the order for them to be presented and the performance measures to be reported under each key success factor.

Once this has been agreed upon, you then need to establish the site standard for displaying the performance measures, introducing it first to the Site Management Weekly Review Meetings, and then to all the remaining Daily Review Meetings throughout the site.

As you progress with the introduction of standard performance measures throughout the site, thought should be given to establishing a baseline and improvement targets supported by monitoring, reviewing and enhancing the performance measures, so that any corrections to the type or display of measures can be conducted immediately across all the scoreboards.

Note

1. *Reference: Understanding, Measuring, and Improving Overall Equipment Effectiveness* by Ross Kenneth Kennedy Aug 2017 CRC Press.

Chapter 4

Structured Daily Review Meetings – Element 4

Are your daily review meetings held just to comply with policy and gather data to feed up the line or are they really focused on ensuring your Frontline Leaders are getting the support they need to safely achieve the production plan each day to the required standard?

Most sites have daily review meetings; however, far too often they are not effective. They start late or drag on for too long, they accept poor performance standards, they skip over below-target performance by accepting 'work-around' corrective actions, they have no agreed triggers for initiating Frontline Problem-Solving Root Cause Analysis and follow-up to issues raised is often just done on an ad-hoc basis if done at all, with very poor monitoring or closure.

Depending on the size and complexity of the site, there will be several layers or tiers of Daily Review Meetings with the information flowing from the lowest level up to the top level.

Ideally the top-level meeting, e.g. Site Daily Review Meeting, should be established first so that the performance measurement framework and standard for all Daily Review Meetings can be set and demonstrated before cascading to the lower levels. This also ensures if an issue at a lower level meeting needs to be escalated to a higher level meeting, the meeting will be able to effectively address the issue.

In reality, as we have introduced effective daily review meetings we found that we get more traction by starting at a mid-level where the impact can be quite impressive, which encourages the existing site level meeting to review and enhance what they are doing. Once the mid-level meetings are effective, we then and only then, tackle the bottom level or Start of Shift level meetings.

As mentioned previously, the role of support staff at Daily Review Meetings is critical and as such before starting we strongly recommend you create a possible plan for all Daily Review Meeting and other support department meetings to ensure there will not be any conflict in timing as you roll out your Daily Review Meetings.

At one site we found the Maintenance Department was holding their weekly review meeting at the same time as the Production Supervisor or Level 1 Salary person was conducting their Packing Area Daily Review Meeting which required the maintenance support person for the Packing Area to attend. The result was that on Fridays the maintenance person would not attend the Packing Area Daily Review Meeting as they were required by their manager to attend the Maintenance Department meeting. Once this was identified it was easy to adjust the timing of one of the meetings so there was no conflict.

Naming of Your Daily Review Meetings

Establishing a naming system for your Daily Review Meetings may seem minor however it can lead to confusion if not properly thought out. We have come across various systems used by different companies, especially when the site is part of a corporate group involving many sites. It is a bit like the names used for different levels in the organisation. One corporate client we worked with who had acquired a number of different sites over time found that using terms like team leader, supervisor and co-ordinator referred to different levels depending on the site, so they decided to create a generic reference to stop confusion. Level 0 was the working Frontline Leader on wages. Level 1 Salary was the first salary position, followed by Level 2 Salary being the next level of salary position. This has led to our original model for Daily Review Meetings being Level 0 or Start of Shift Meetings and Level 1 being the Daily Review Meeting conducted by the Level 1 Salary person, and so on up the levels. However, when visiting sites not familiar to our approach we have come across reference to Tiers for Daily Review Meetings where the Tier 1 meeting is the Start of Shift Meeting conducted by the wages Frontline Leader and Tier 2 is conducted by the Level 1 Salary person. At the end of the day if you are a standalone site which system you use doesn't really matter. However, if you are part of a multi-site organisation we would suggest there is agreement across the sites to use one description method to stop confusion (Figures 4.1 and 4.2).

We have come across some sites where they started at the bottom and established Tier 1 or Level 0 Start of Shift Meetings because there was no effective Tier 2 or Level 1 Meetings. As issues from the Start of Shift Meetings needed to be escalated, they tended to go into a 'black hole' of inactivity resulting in very frustrated Frontline Leaders.

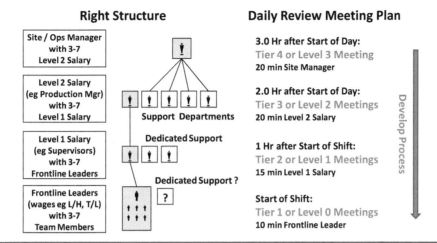

Figure 4.1   Developing a daily review meeting plan for a large site.

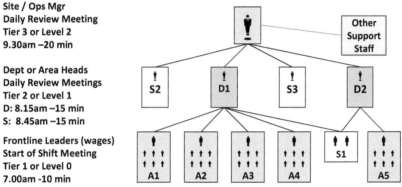

Figure 4.2   Developing a detailed daily review meeting plan for a small site.

What Should Be the Reason and Purpose of a Daily Review Meeting?

Before initiating a Daily Review Meeting Plan there should be a consensus from the participants as to the purpose of each meeting. Sadly, many sites see the primary reason of a Daily Review Meeting is to collect information for reporting to high levels, rather than seeing them as a means to further develop and support their people. Collecting information for reporting is certainly necessary; however, making this the secondary reason, to the primary reason of developing and supporting people, will have a more significant positive impact on operational performance than just focusing on collecting information for reporting above.

Below is an example purpose of a Daily Review Meeting:

1. Review the previous day of operations by area or line (Performance Board and Trend Run Charts) by exception and allocate action items or root cause analysis if required

2. Confirm any changes to production plan or work plan for next 24–48 hours and identify and address any issues that may impact the next day of operations
3. Review Action Board – update with new actions and report on any overdue or completed actions
4. Review Root Cause Analysis Board and Triggers Listing – allocate or feedback on progress of Frontline Problem-Solving Root Cause Analysis
5. Review Parking Lot/Escalation Board – update with new issues and report progress of any existing issues
6. Communications update – feedback from previous higher level Daily Review Meeting, any visits to site/area today etc.
7. Roundtable – any other issues to ensure everyone leaves knowing they have sufficient support to achieve their plan

What Makes an Effective Daily Review Meeting?

Too often we come across what we would term ineffective Daily Review Meetings where targets have not been meet and all that gets discussed are excuses and work-arounds, where the same issues continue to re-emerge, or where people walk away mumbling that the meeting was a waste of their time.

Below is a listing of some of the features you may wish to consider for your Daily Review Meetings:

1. Location is appropriate for the meeting
2. Stand-up environment as people think and respond quicker and more distinctly on their feet
3. No access to coffee facilities or vending machines as it's too tempting of a distraction
4. Agenda with timeframes is displayed
5. Clock is visible to all and is visually controlling the time of meeting
6. Meeting starts and finishes on time to allow people to leave after agreed finish time
7. Issues are raised but not solved with problem solving conducted outside the meeting
8. Current performances updated by responsible attendees and displayed using visual prompts (e.g. black is target, green is good, red is bad)
9. Tier 2 and 3 or Level 1 and 2 Meetings focus on area or line total performance rather than separate metric performances
10. Focus is on helping Area Leaders at Tier 3 or Level 2 Meetings and Frontline Leaders at Tier 2 or Level 1 Meetings to address their concerns

Points 9 and 10, if applied correctly, can make a significant impact on the effectiveness of the Daily Review Meeting in developing your Frontline Leaders which needs to be considered when formatting your meeting agenda.

What Information Should Be Reported at Daily Review Meeting?

The information reported will often be dependent on what tier or level the meeting is addressing. For example, we often ask the following question when determining the information to be reported:

What Information Does the Production Manager Require on a Daily Basis?

Examples of responses to this question includes:

- What happened during the previous day of operations that has had an effect on the Production Plan?
  - Have we had any safety concerns?
  - Have we made any scrap or rework?
  - Have we had any breakdowns?
  - Have we had a full crew?
- Have we got the parts and materials to make our Production Plan today?
- Are there any foreseen blockages that may stop the Production Plan being achieved today or tomorrow?
- Have we found any opportunities to improve?

Selecting Performance Measures for Review at a Daily Review Meeting

Appropriate measures and targets that will drive the desired behaviours should be established under each Key Success Factor for Operations and reported by designated area or line, by the person responsible for that area or line on a 'by exemption' basis, e.g. if its reported green (made or above expectation) then there is no need to discuss, whereas if reported red (below expectation) then there is a need to explain why and what is being done about it. The sequence they are reporting should be based on the agreed order of the site's Key Success Factors for Operations.

Key Success Factors for Operations	Possible Performance Measures
Safety and Environment	Accidents (injury to person) Incidents (damage to equipment or environment) Near miss accident or incident (if being reported)
Quality	Scrap Rework generated Yield loss Internal complaints – quality, delivery etc.

Key Success Factors for Operations	Possible Performance Measures
Customer Satisfaction	Achievement of Production Plan Stability of the Production Plan – number of changes, cancelled or deferred events External complaints – quality, delivery etc.
Plant and Equipment	Equipment failure or work-around Changeovers taking longer than standard Equipment defects found and rectified
People	Attendance Unplanned absenteeism Productivity
Supplier	Quality issues Delivery issues
Inventory	Shortages Excesses

Developing the Format and Agenda of a Daily Review Meeting

There are several formats that a Daily Review Meeting can take. The most common is where the chair works through the agenda and asks the relevant persons to comment on each item. For example, the meeting may start with safety so anyone may speak up, but most of the time the only comments will come from the safety representative. Next may be quality so again anyone may speak up, but most of the time the only comments will come from the quality representative. Next might be customer satisfaction or delivery so again anyone may speak up, but most of the time the only comments will come from the customer services representative.

An example of such an agenda found on display when visiting a site is shown in Table 4.1.

This format may be effective in collecting the relevant information required to be reported up the line, however it does not place accountability on leaders for their area of responsibility across the critical Key Success Factors for Operations.

A more effective format that promotes ownership, accountability and development of the leaders of the specific areas is to structure the agenda so each Area Leader reports on the critical Key Success Factors within their area of responsibility as demonstrated in the agenda is show in Table 4.2.

The above agenda is based on three production areas being reported on. At some sites it may also include the warehouse or logistics (goods in and out) area. At larger sites the number of areas involved could be increased. At some sites where maintenance plays a significant role, the Maintenance Leader would report

Table 4.1   Example of a Poorly Constructed Daily Review Meeting Agenda

Daily Review Meeting Agenda found on display when visiting a site	
Item	*Activity*
1.	**Safety & Environment** Any accidents, incidents or near misses during previous day
2.	**Achievement of Production Plan** Any misses to expected plan by Production Area by exception • Throughput • If production target was met (what worked) • If production target was not met (what needs to be done to hit the daily throughput) • Downtime
3.	**Statistical Process Control (SPC) Checks** • Amount of product checked • Amount of product failed
4.	**Daily Scrap Figures** • Top 3 reasons for scrapping material • Do we have enough people for the next 24 hours to achieve the plan?
5.	**Non-Conformance Reports (again using their language – it is Non-Conformance Reports (an actual document generated when there is a quality problem) Reported**
6.	**Absenteeism and Planned Leave**
7.	**Reactive Problem Solving (to be done outside the meeting)** • Status of all outstanding Frontline Problem-Solving Root Cause Analysis activities
8.	**Production Issues** • When they were raised • Person who raised the issue
9.	**Review Action List**
10.	**Upcoming Events**

Note: Information boards to be updated during the meeting. This meeting is not to solve problems. It is to discuss the previous day and plan for today's success.

the same as the Production Leaders covering the first five items and hence eliminating the need for item 9.

Initially the person responsible for the meeting will chair the meeting to demonstrate how this is done. For example, at a Tier 3 or Level 2 Daily Review Meeting the Production Level 2 Salary person (e.g. Production Manager) would initially chair the meeting with the Area Leaders reporting. Once the standard for the meeting has been set, we recommended each Area Leader would do a week of chairing to 'learn by doing', then the Level 2 Salary person would chair again for a week to further demonstrate the required standard, then the Area Leaders would again do weekly rotations. The aim is to develop the skills and confidence of the Area Leaders so they can improve the way they lead their Tier 2 or Level 1

Table 4.2 Example of a Properly Constructed Daily Review Meeting Agenda

Tier 3 or Level 2 Daily Review Meeting Agenda that Promotes Ownership and Area Leader Development			
Item	*Activity*	*Who*	*Time*
1.	**Safety and Environment** • Any injuries, incidents or near misses during the previous day • Any issues or concerns for today	Area 1 Leader / Area 2 Leader / Area 3 Leader	2 min × 3 = 6 min
2.	**Quality (Internal)** • Any losses or issues (e.g. Non-Conformance Reports raised) during the previous day • Any issues or concerns for today		
3.	**Delivery – Achievement of Production Plan** • Did we make the output we planned to do during the previous day? • Are we on track to make the output we have planned for today?		
4.	**Plant and Equipment** • Any issues with plant & equipment during the previous day (breakdowns, extended changeovers, delays) • Any issues or concerns with plant & equipment which will impact performance today		
5.	**People** • Did we have enough people during the previous day to achieve the plan? • Do we have enough people for today to achieve the plan?		
6.	**Customer Satisfaction (External)** • Any customer complaints, issues	Customer Service	1 min
7.	**Planning and Scheduling Stability** • Any changes or shortages	Prod Planning	1 min
8.	**Logistics Issues** • Any storage, shortages, delays, concerns	Logistics	1 min
9.	**Maintenance Issues** • Any issues from yesterday, planned outages	Maintenance	1 min
10.	**Improvement Activities** • Did we achieve our improvement plan for the previous day (did we have to cancel or defer any activity/event)? • What is the improvement plan for today (and rest of week or next week)?	Improvement Co-ordinator	1 min

(Continued)

Table 4.2 (Continued) Example of a Properly Constructed Daily Review Meeting Agenda

Item	Activity	Who	Time
11.	**Review Action Board and Parking Lot Board**	Chair	1 min
12.	**Review Root Cause Analysis** • What is the status of all outstanding RCA analysis?	Chair	1 min
13.	**Communications Update** • Any visitors to site	All	1 min
14.	**Issues of Concern** • Any further issues or concerns	All	1 min
		Total Time:	**15 min**

Note: Information boards to be updated before the meeting by the responsible persons. Action List Board and Root Cause Analysis Board to be updated during the meeting.

Daily Review Meetings, or be prepared to competently lead their Daily Review Meetings when they are initiated.

Determining the Rules for a Daily Review Meeting

It is important there are agreed rules for each Daily Review Meeting that are on display and adhered to by all attendees. Some sites impose a consequence such as putting a $1 or $2 coin in the charity jar, if a rule is broken to encourage, in a fun way, respect and discipline for the rules. Below is an example of possible rules for a Daily Review Meeting:

■ Meeting to start and finish on time
■ Attendees may leave after nominated finish time if meeting extends past agreed finish time
■ Agenda to be followed
■ All required information to be updated on information boards before the start time of the meeting using agreed colour coding
■ Mobile phones to be in silent mode – urgent calls only to be taken outside the meeting
■ Problem solving of issues raised to be done outside meeting
■ Agreed triggers to be used to escalate issues/incidents that have not been resolved to Frontline Problem-Solving Root Cause Analysis (see Chapter 6) with set timeframes for initial report back of proposed solutions to address the root causes
■ Respect for all personnel at all times
■ Only one person talking at any time with a loud clear voice

Setting Triggers and Policies to Initiate Frontline Problem-Solving Root Cause Analysis

Too often issues/incidents reported at Daily Review Meetings which have occurred in the previous 24 hours, are backed up by a report of a successful work-around.

Reported Issue: motor bearing failed due to contamination getting into the grease
Reported Action: we were able to replace motor with only minimal plant downtime

What is not reported (or addressed) is the root cause for the issue (grease being contaminated). Hence, there is a need to identify when only a work-around is reported and establish a process of initiating Frontline Problem-Solving Root Cause Analysis – otherwise the issue may happen again in say 6–12 months' time.

So as not to overload your people, triggers for initiating Frontline Problem-Solving Root Cause Analysis need to be set and displayed along with policies on how many root cause analyses can be conducted by a person simultaneously.

Example triggers for a site just starting their reactive improvement journey using the Key Success Factor for Operations framework

Key Success Factors for Operations	Possible Triggers
Safety and Environment	• Any accident • Any incident causing damage to equipment or facilities • Any reportable environment incident • Any environment incident requiring greater than 30 min to clean-up
Quality	• Scrap or rework loss of greater than 5% from a line • Yield loss of greater than 5% above standard from a line • Internal customer quality complaint of agreed value
Customer Satisfaction	• Any external customer complaint caused by operations • Production Plan miss by greater than 10%
Plant and Equipment	• Breakdown causing production delay of over 1 hour duration • Any 'work-around' implemented to keep the plant running • Replacing a key piece of equipment (e.g. pump) outside of its scheduled replacement time
People	• Productivity down greater than 10% • Unplanned absenteeism greater than 10%
Supplier	• Delivery problem that impacted Production Plan • Quality problem that impacted Production Plan
Inventory	• Any shortage that impacted Production Plan

Note: Best practice would be to address any of the above events.

Example policies for a site just starting their Reactive Improvement journey

Purpose: What are we trying to achieve?	To set guidelines as to when a Frontline Problem-Solving Root Cause Analysis using the Frontline Problem-Solving 7-Step Process is to be initiated, and by whom
Scope: Who is this aimed for?	Daily review meeting attendees
Policy Statement: When something happens, what to do, by when and by who	Triggers are to be set for relevant measures within the site's Key Success Factors for Operations framework and displayed in the Information Centre where the daily review meeting is conducted. Triggers are to be reviewed at least every 6 months and adjusted by a minimum of 10% A person can only be allocated one Frontline Problem-Solving Root Cause Analysis at a time until the proposed actions are identified and agreed. Once an agreed trigger is identified, the responsible person for the trigger (e.g. at a Level 2 Daily Review Meeting would be the Level 1 Salary person responsible for the issue/problem) will be allocated (by the chair of the Daily Review Meeting) the task of completing a Frontline Problem-Solving Root Cause Analysis with an agreed timeframe to report back the outcomes from the root cause analysis along with outlining proposed actions for approval at the designated Daily Review Meeting. Once the proposed actions are approved, then the responsible person will ensure the actions are implemented within the agreed timeframe. The completed Frontline Problem-Solving A3 Summary Sheet is to be presented back to the Daily Review Meeting for sharing the learning and sign-off for completeness by the chair of the Daily Review Meeting. The completed Frontline Problem-Solving A3 Summary Sheet is then to be filed by the Improvement Co-ordinator in the sites central improvement knowledge base (e.g. directory on server) using the site's equipment structure framework.

Start of Shift Review Meeting

Typically, this meeting is conducted by the Frontline Leader and involves all their crew or direct reports.

The purpose of the Start of Shift Review Meeting, apart from being a muster call to ensure everyone has arrived on time and ready for work, should be to:

■ Review previous day's performance (what can we learn or what specials actions we need to follow-up);

- Review what will impact today's performance; and
- Provide a brief communication update.

Typically, the meeting is no longer than 10 minutes and is conducted by the Frontline Leader involving all their crew or direct reports. If the Frontline Leader is not available, then the second-in-charge should conduct the meeting. The meeting should also assist the Frontline Leader in preparing for the Tier 2 or Level 1 Daily Review Meeting they will be attending (Table 4.3).

The agenda should be established with the Frontline Leader and tailored to suit their area of responsibility. The agenda should be regularly reviewed and updated as new learning occurs.

Table 4.3   Example Start of Shift Review Meeting Agenda Conducted by the Frontline Leader

Item	Activity	Time
1.	**Review previous day's performance – refer Performance Board** • Any near misses yesterday we can learn from? • Any quality issues that need follow-up? • Any problems with our machines/equipment? • Any component shortages that need follow-up?	3 min
2.	**Review today's expectations – refer Production Planning Board** • Do we all know where we are working today? • Do we know our production requirements for today? • Do we need to do any preparation today for tomorrow's production plan?	3 min
3.	**Improvement Activities** • Did we achieve our improvement plan for yesterday • What is our improvement plan for today (and rest of week)	1 min
4.	**Review Action Board and Parking Lot Board**	1 min
5.	**Communications Update** Provide feedback from previous Tier 2 or Level 1 Daily Review Meeting attended Advise any external visitors to site/area	1 min
6.	Issues of Concern • **Any further issues or concerns**	1 min
	Total Time:	**10 min**

Notes: Performance Board to be updated before the meeting.
Production Planning Board to be updated before the meeting.
Action Board to be updated during the meeting.

Chapter 5

Visual Information Centres – Element 5

Are information boards used to allow everyone to see at a glance where the problems are, and what is being done about them, or do people have to search through screens of information to get an understanding of the situation?

Information Centres are places where Daily Review Meetings are conducted. Ideally, they should be located where the people who work in the area can see them clearly. Depending on the type of site, the Information Centres may be located in a space or on a wall near the work area or a place where everyone walks past, however if noise or other distracting environmental conditions exist, then they may need to be located in a room preferably with significant glass walls or windows for people to see as they walk past.

Some sites refer to their Information Centres as WAR rooms:

Work	We review and reflect on our Work
Action	We take Action where expectations are not met
Results	We get the Results we deserve

Others call them Pulse rooms – the heartbeat of operations. What you call them really depends on the site; however, the critical thing is to ensure they all follow the agreed site standard for displaying information. This way, as you move through the plant to different areas, the same information will be located in the same place and displayed in the same method e.g. red for missed expectation, green for achieved or exceeded expectation, hand drawn monthly run charts for daily trending, printed 26-week bar charts for weekly trending etc., rather than having run charts in one area, bar charts in another, and pie charts in another etc.

What Should Be Displayed?

Below is a listing of the type of displays we find at Information Centres:

- Meeting agenda
- Scoreboard of daily performance to monitor achievement to expectation with provision for comments if expectations are missed
- Monthly run charts of daily performance for the key performance measures to monitor trending
- Planning Board to monitor achievement to expectation in units and to advise tomorrow's plan
- Action list
- Policies for Frontline Problem-Solving Root Cause Analysis
- Triggers for Frontline Problem-Solving Root Cause Analysis
- Root Cause Analysis Status Board
- Parking Lot Board to capture issues that need to be escalated to a higher-level meeting
- Clock with visual control to monitor the timing of the meeting
- Marker pen holder with at least two of each required colour, along with a whiteboard wiper for cleaning the boards before entering the next day's data

Setting Up Your Information Centres

Some sites like to go straight into permanently marked up whiteboards, often with company logo and fancy headings. Our experience is to start with a simpler and more flexible approach that allows easy adjustments and changes until the right measures and information reported is agreed to by all. We have found this can often take several weeks. As such, the simpler approach we use is to design up the key sheets on a computer then print them on A3 size paper and laminate them, so they can be written if required, as in the case of the Scoresheet, with a whiteboard marker then easily wiped clean ready for the next day's reporting. The sheets can then be placed on a wall or whiteboard and moved around as required. When changes are made, it is very easy to print off the updated sheet, laminate it and replace the old sheet. Once the final design is agreed, a permanent marked up whiteboard can be established.

Another important aspect of designing an Information Centre is the ownership by the participants. This is best demonstrated in the case study below.

CASE STUDY 1: FROM COMPLIANCE TO PASSION

Too often Daily Review Meetings become a compliance exercise ... *"Yes boss, we had our meeting and here are the figures"* ... rather than a process of developing your supervisors and Frontline Leaders.

This was the challenge at one site where corporate had prescribed the meeting agenda and provided the standard reporting information boards only to have the Production Manager, Production Supervisors and Support Staff attend their morning meeting at 9.45 am and just tick all the boxes. They would finish the meeting within 5–10 minutes with little said by many, and only the occasional note taken down in someone's notebook if a task needed to be done.

The site was part of a large company providing high quality laundry services for the food and beverage and accommodation industry, along with an extensive range of industrial garments and floor mats for organisations including medical, retail, manufacturing and mining.

Each day the site receives many truckloads of linen and garments that need to be sorted, washed, ironed and folded, and made ready for delivery the next day. With a workforce of over 50 people, which can include more than 20% casual employees depending on the season, Effective Daily Management can be a daunting challenge.

During discussions with the Branch General Manager, it was identified that due to the challenges of providing very short turn-arounds for their quality-focused customers, Effective Daily Management was essential; however, he felt there was opportunity for significant improvement across all levels of the business.

It was agreed the Tier 3 or Level 2 Daily Review Process headed by the Production Manager (Level 2 Salary) would be the best starting point to develop the supervisors (Level 1 Salary) so they could then enhance their Level 1 Daily Review Meetings with their Leading Hands and crews.

Over a 9-week period the team of eight, led by the Production Manager with the Branch General Manager as one of the team members along with all the Production Supervisors and key Support Staff, worked through a 9-step process which involved two 2-hour meetings over the first 2 weeks, followed by 1-hour weekly meetings for the remaining 7 weeks.

After forming into a team and being given an overview of the seven key elements of Reactive Improvement to achieve Effective Daily Management, they developed a baseline for their current performance using two rating sheets:

■ The daily management innocence to excellence rating covering the seven elements which they scored 51%; and
■ The Daily Review Meeting rating which they scored 62%.

Next came their vision for a Level 2 Daily Review Meeting along with its purpose and desired attributes before determining what information they needed to report each day and how it should be displayed. Through consensus, they soon mapped out an entirely different approach to their daily meeting.

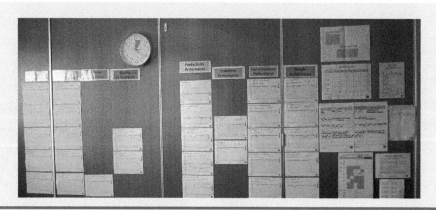

Figure 5.1   Daily Review Meeting trial Information Centre.

They moved the meeting from their previous location of the lunch room in the factory to the admin training room where there was more space for creating their trial Information Centre and made it easier for the key support people to attend (Figure 5.1).

Issues raised were now being listed on an action list for all to see and reviewed daily to ensure prompt actions. Once the Production Manager set the standard for chairing the meeting, each Supervisor rotated weekly in chairing, to develop their skills and confidence to take to their Level 1 Daily Review Meetings with their Leading Hands and crews (Figure 5.2).

After 9 weeks they re-rated themselves, the daily management seven elements rating increased from 51% to 80% or a *57% improvement*, and the Daily Review Meeting rating increased from 62% to 93% or a *50% improvement*.

As stated by one Supervisor, 'the passion has come back to the workplace where we are all trying to help each other to have a good day'.

Figure 5.2   Initial Daily Review Meeting in action.

Once the Daily Review Meeting has been conducted for say a month, hopefully with formal reviews conducted each week with all participants, and a month of daily run chart data collected, a decision can be made with confidence to introduce permanently marked-up boards where appropriate (Figures 5.3 through 5.6).

One of the most important parts of an Information Centre is the action list, however in many situations we find it is hardly used. When investigated further, we found many attendees believe that because the problem that resulted in a miss in performance was corrected there was no need to put an action on the action list. Upon hearing this we adjusted the heading on the action list to include the words 'to stop problems/issues happening again'. This provided an excellent prompt for the chair of the meeting to keep asking this question every time an expected performance was not achieved (Figure 5.7).

Scoreboard to be updated before the meeting by person responsible

Date of Meeting: **Date being Reviewed:**

Key Success Factors	Measures	Targets	Line 1	Line 2	Line 3	Reasons for Misses (Red)
Safety & Environment	Number of Injuries (harm)	0				
	Number of Incidents (damage)	0				
Quality	Scrap Units	0				
	Rework Hrs	0				
Customer Satisfaction	Customer Complaints	0				
	Achievement of Prod Plan	100%				
Plant & Equipment	Unplanned Downtime Mins	15				
	OEE	82%				
People	Unplanned Absentees Yesterday	0				
	Unplanned Absentees Today	0				
Inventory	Shortages	0				

Black – Targets, Green – Achieved, Red – Missed

Target:	■	Achieved:	▢	Missed	▨

Figure 5.3   **Example Daily Review Meeting performance scoreboard.**

Safety & Environment	Quality (Internal)	Customer Satisfaction	Plant & Equipment	People
Line 1				
Injuries	Scrap	Good Output	OEE	Output / Mins worked
Incidents	Rework	Misses to Plan	Unplanned Downtime	Unplanned Absentees
Line 2				
Injuries	Scrap	Good Output	OEE	Output / Mins worked
Incidents	Rework	Misses to Plan	Unplanned Downtime	Unplanned Absentees

- All charts to be set-up with measurement definitions such that trending up is good and trending down is bad, so that it is easy to interpret as people walk past
- When filling in each chart, suggest colour coding is used eg **Black** – Targets, Green – Achieved, Red – Missed
- Charts should be updated before the meeting by the person responsible

Figure 5.4   Example daily run charts to monitor trends.

Safety & Environment: Injuries

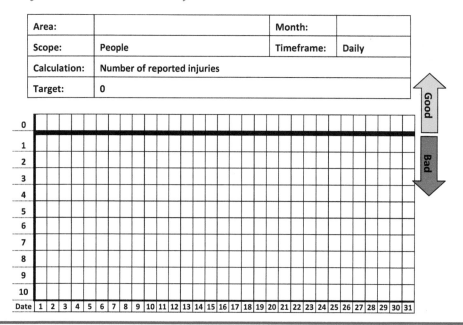

Figure 5.5   Example run chart – safety and environment: injuries.

Line	Product	Previous Day Plan	Previous Day Actual	Today Plan	Next Day Plan	Reason for Miss / Comments
1						
2						
3						

Figure 5.6   Example planning board.

to stop problems / issues happening again

Date	Area	Raised By	Action Required	Assigned To	Target Date	Revised Date	Status	Comments

Figure 5.7   Example Daily Review Meeting action list.

Date	Area	Concern	What	When	Who	Status	Completed

Figure 5.8   Example layout of basic concern strip

Some sites that we visit like to use concern strips to monitor the status of their actions in addressing problems or issues; however, we find unless there is good discipline and understanding the strips can become overwhelming and distractive to those attending Daily Review Meetings for the first time. Once the Daily Review Meeting is properly established and working well, concern strips can be introduced if desired. They do provide the flexibility of easily prioritising the order by being moveable rather than rubbing out and rewriting information. The strips are normally made with a whiteboard material front and magnetic backing so they can be used on a metal backing board.

Example Layout of Basic Concern Strip

Once Daily Review Meetings and Information Centres are well established, the next phase of developing your daily management activities would be to introduce Frontline Problem-Solving Root Cause Analysis as outlined in Chapter 6. To support this, the Information Centre will need to be expanded to include triggers, policies and a status board for your Frontline Problem-Solving Root Cause Analysis activities. Triggers and policies were outlined in Chapter 4, and in Chapter 6 we cover in detail a development program to train your people in conducting Frontline Problem-Solving Root Cause Analysis (Figure 5.10).

At this stage, if you are using concern strips, you may wish to enhance them to support your Frontline Problem-Solving Root Cause Analysis by redesigning

Date	Area	Concern	Contain-ment	When	Counter-measure	Who	Target	Status	Completed		
										2	3	4
									5	6	7	

Figure 5.9   Example layout of a root cause analysis concern strip

Date	Area	RCA Description	Assigned To	Target Date Analysis & Solutions	Revised Date Analysis & Solutions	Target Date Completed	Revised Date Completed	Status / Comments

Figure 5.10   Example Root Cause Analysis Status Board.

them with a Plan-Do-Check-Act or P-D-C-A wheel so you can colour in as you progress around the wheel, along with provision to mark which step you are up to in the Root Cause Analysis process.

Example Layout of a Root Cause Analysis Concern Strip

Finally, we have found it helpful for Daily Review Meetings if they have a Parking Lot Board or Escalation Board to allow issues that are not appropriate to be addressed at the time, due to time constraints or are outside the boundaries of the team, to be parked for a future meeting or escalated to a higher Level or Tier Daily Review Meeting or Management Team. This way the issue is noted on the board and can be addressed at a later meeting or reported back on by the chair of the meeting after it has been escalated (Figure 5.11).

Issues to be:
A ☑: To be addressed in future
B ☑: To be escalated to higher Daily Review Meeting
C ☑: To be referred to Management Team

Date	A ☑	B ☑	C ☑	Description of Issue	Date Actioned

Figure 5.11   Example Daily Review Meeting Parking Lot Board.

CASE STUDY 2: ADDRESSING THE THREE CRITICAL PARTS OF YOUR CONTINUOUS IMPROVEMENT STRATEGY

The trilogy of tackling reactive improvement, stabilising the Production Plan through flow logic, and pro-active improvement combine together to give synergistic results.

The site has been manufacturing Personal Protective Equipment (PPE) products such as safety helmets, face protection and hearing protection for over 70 years.

After commencing their continuous improvement (CI) journey with two improvement teams each focused on a bottleneck production area, the Management Team wanted to maintain their momentum by introducing a further three improvement teams with each team, like their first cycle teams, taking part in two 2 hour kick-off workshops followed by weekly 1 hour meetings spanning 12 weeks so as to minimise disruption to production, while having sufficient time to achieve their mandate.

The first improvement team was focused on Reactive Improvement. This team was established to develop a Start of Shift Review Meeting in the plants moulding area.

The team established a very effective Start of Shift Review Meeting where any performance issues could be captured and acted on so they did not occur again. In the past a lot of things got talked about, however there was no formal way to follow-up the issues and often they would repeat (Figure 5.12).

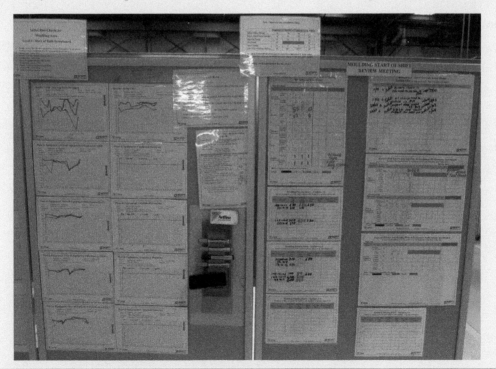

Figure 5.12   **Start of Shift Review Meeting Information Centre.**

The team was also able to identify several improvements that they implemented throughout the cycle including improving the accuracy of component counts which was an issue for production planning and the retail packaging area.

The second improvement team was focused on stabilising the Production Plan through flow logic. The Production Planning Team tackled this issue by conducting a Glenday Sieve analysis of all active SKUs (Stock Keeping Units). However, they soon realised it would be better to divide the active SKUs into product groups and focus on the dominant product group – safety helmets.

By also introducing Base Assembly Rationalisation thinking, they were able to create a Green Stream Fixed Sequence Fixed Time Schedule for two of the four helmet moulding machines that minimised set-up time, colour changes and material changes for more than 50% of helmet production.

The third improvement team was focused on pro-active improvement. A Cross-functional Macro Focused Equipment &Process Improvement Team (refer to *Understanding, Measuring and Improving Overall Equipment Effectiveness* Chapter 4: Improving OEE, which explains how these types of team go about their improvement activities) was established in the pad printing area where multi-coloured customer logos are printed onto safety helmets (Figure 5.13).

As the team analysed their current situation through operator surveys, Operator Knowledge Base Analysis, and observations supported by performance data, they were able to identify a number of key issues that had emerged including variability in ink, condition of rings, plates, pads, and jigs.

As the team progressed through each opportunity, performance in the area improved as highlighted on their Daily Review Meeting Information Centre.

The overall success of the teams in Cycle 2 saw:

■ > 10% reduction in material waste for the pad printing and moulding areas; and
■ > 10% increase in capacity for the pad printing and moulding areas.

Figure 5.13   **Part of the pad printing area.**

Commitment to CI by the teams was also demonstrated by:

■ Start of Shift Review Meeting Team working with the Production Planning Team to create inventory monitoring run charts to support the Green Stream Production Plan; and
■ Pad Printing Team provided regular feedback to the Production Planning Team regarding helmet quality issues affecting their printing to ensure the new Fix Sequence Fix Time Plan addressed their issues.

As stated by one area co-ordinator, 'by being in a team environment and systematically understanding all the variables impacting on our performance, we have had good buy-in to introduce changes in a previously set-way work environment'.

Chapter 6

Frontline Problem-Solving Root Cause Analysis Capability – Element 6

Have you developed the problem-solving skills of all your frontline people so that if there is an incident that triggers a root cause analysis, they commence the root cause analysis before the daily review meeting rather than wait for someone to tell them to do it?

A frontline problem is an event or incident that stops the shift from achieving one of its performance expectations or targets, for example quality expectation down due to a pallet of rework or scrap, or output below expectation due to a breakdown. It is not a trend of poor performance over time, or a gap in the benchmark to other best practices, for example our set-ups take 40 minutes when they should be 10 minutes. These poor performance trends and gaps in benchmarks should be addressed through pro-active improvement using a 9-step process as outlined in *Understanding, Measuring and Improving Overall Equipment Effectiveness*.

In Frontline problem solving it is also important to remember what some refer to as the 'Tyranny of Time'. The longer the time between a problem or incident occurring, and the time you discover it, the more difficult and more expensive it will be to solve as evidence, especially people's memories, decay with time. For example, asking someone what happened 5 minutes ago compared to asking them what happened yesterday, will often give you vastly different responses.

Steven J Spear, a senior lecturer at the MIT Sloan School of Management reinforces this thinking in his award-winning and critically acclaimed book, *The High Velocity Edge,* where he states: 'the longer the problem remains unresolved, the more difficult and more expensive it will be to solve'.

There are two fundamental aspects of Reactive Improvement:

1. Reacting immediately so that the overall process returns to normal conditions as soon as possible; and
2. Frontline problem solving so as to find and take action on the root cause or causes of the problem, including those that can be managed at the least expense of cost and time.

The aim of Frontline Problem-Solving Root Cause Analysis is to focus on item 2 above, recognising that by becoming competent in this you will also develop the ability to carry out item 1 more effectively and the number of problems or incidents occurring should reduce significantly.

There are many Root Cause Analysis problem-solving processes in the marketplace; however, the key (as discovered by Toyota many years ago) to Operational Excellence is to find one that can be used by all people in the organisation rather than just a select few.

A problem-solving process should be more than just solving problems and getting things done. It needs to be able to:

■ Create problem solvers at all levels in the company especially those people who add the value to your output;
■ Create an environment where problem solving is valued and promoted as a means to develop and unleash the full potential of all people in your company; and
■ Create a learning organisation through the use of Frontline Problem-Solving Root Cause Analysis A3 Summary Sheets to capture and share the learning of your people.

Toyota saying ... "No Problem Is a Problem"

Over the past 20 years we have been developing a simple but highly effective 7 Step Frontline Problem-Solving Root Cause Analysis Process based on the use of detailed problem definition, cause & effect analysis and why-why analysis that is now being successfully used by many organisations at all levels.

The process can be based on the Plan-Do-Check-Act (P-D-C-A) scientific method of problem solving which involves a continuous progression of:

■ Developing a hypothesis (understanding what is causing the problem);
■ Testing the hypothesis (taking corrective action to rectify the problem);
■ Measuring results (to verify the problem has been rectified); if required
■ Adjusting the hypothesis (based on learning from initial test);
■ Retesting the hypothesis; and
■ Measuring results and so forth until the desired result is achieved (Figure 6.1).

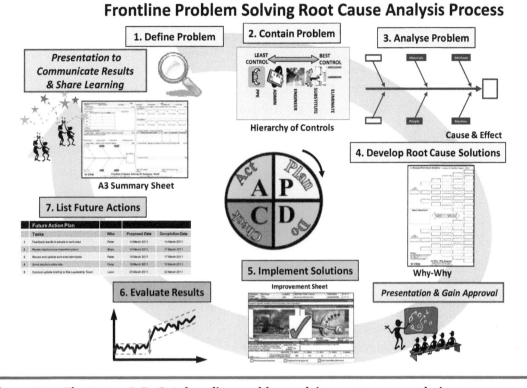

Figure 6.1 **The 7 step P-D-C-A frontline problem-solving root cause analysis process.**

PLAN: Understand the Problem and Develop an Action Plan

Activities may include:

- **Define Problem** by creating a Problem Statement and specification (Step 1)
- **Contain Problem** by taking immediate actions or counter-measures to contain the consequences of the problem (Step 2)
- **Analyse problem** through data gathering, along with cause & effect analysis (Step 3)
- **Develop root cause solutions** and an action plan to permanently fix the problem (Step 4)
- Gain approval for the action plan

DO: Implement Solutions (the Action Plan) (Step 5)

Activities may include:

- Conducting trials, experiments, pilots or changes
- Identifying additional improvement opportunities as you are implementing the Action Plan

CHECK: Evaluate Results (Step 6)

Activities may include:

■ Collecting actual process data after the change and arrange the data the same way you originally defined the problem (i.e. charting)
■ Reintroducing the root cause to see if the problem comes back (acid test)
■ Comparing the results to baseline data to verify the improvement has been effective and sustaining

ACT: List Future Actions (Step 7)

Activities may include:

■ Refining the solutions by re-commencing the P-D-C-A cycle if the desired result is not achieved
■ Locking in the solutions by standardising through:
  – Updating work instructions or methods and standard operating procedures
  – Conducting training
  – Applying mistake proofing
■ Make recommendations for further improvement activities
■ Apply solutions or changes elsewhere in the organisation in areas which are experiencing similar problems or have similar processes

An alternative approach that some sites prefer to ensure consistency with their Lean/Six Sigma Program is the Define-Measure-Analyse-Improve-Control (D-M-A-I-C) framework for the same seven steps (Figure 6.2).

A key outcome from Frontline Problem-Solving Root Cause Analysis is an A3 Summary Sheet which can be used to share the learning from the analysis and be a record for future reference if a similar problem occurs. A company or site standard for the format and language structure of the A3 Summary Sheet should be established so that each A3 Summary Sheet can be evaluated and any variation to the standard used to further train your people involved.

By having all A3 Summary Sheets to a standard it becomes very easy for everyone to read and interpret the outcomes, and if appropriate to contribute to further learning (Figure 6.3).

Introducing Frontline Problem-Solving Root Cause Analysis

A Frontline Problem-Solving Root Cause Analysis is normally allocated to the responsible person at a daily review meeting following an incident or event that

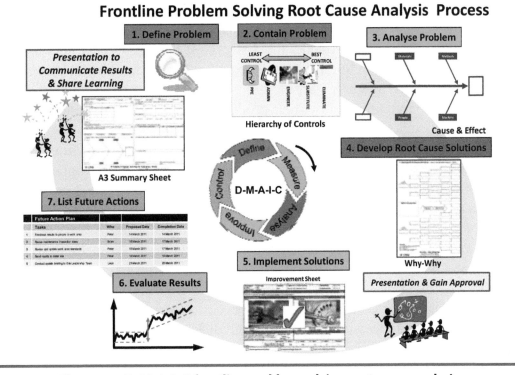

Figure 6.2 The 7 step D-M-A-I-C frontline problem-solving root cause analysis process.

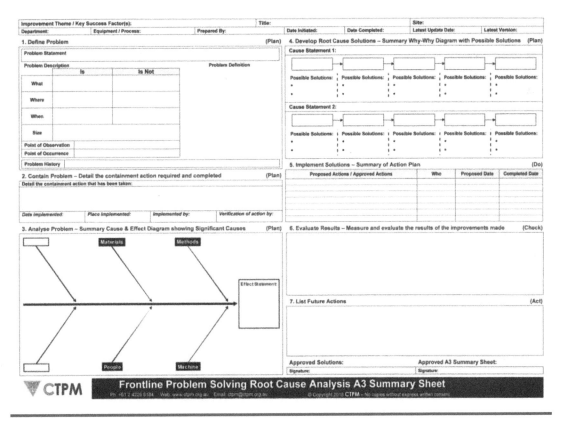

Figure 6.3 Frontline problem-solving root cause analysis A3 summary sheet.

has exceeded a pre-arranged trigger. For example, at the Production Managers Level 2 Daily Review Meeting attended by Level 1 Salary people, a Level 1 Salary person may be allocated to conduct the analysis. At a Level 1 Daily Review Meeting attended by Frontline Leaders, a Frontline Leader may be allocated to conduct the analysis, and at a Start of Shift Review Meeting conducted by the Frontline Leader and attended by their production crew of 3–7 operators, an operator may be allocated to conduct the analysis.

The person allocated would conduct an initial investigation to define the problem and ensure proper Containment then call upon their colleagues to assist in analysing the problem and developing root cause solutions. Once possible solutions are identified they would take the analysis back to their Daily Review Meeting for approval to proceed with the agreed actions.

The key to introducing Frontline Problem-Solving Root Cause Analysis into a workplace is developing an effective implementation process. Often, attending a one- or two-day workshop is a great way to be introduced to Frontline Problem-Solving Root Cause Analysis; however, to learn and gain confidence you often need to successfully work through at least three problems to an agreed standard.

An effective way of achieving this is to undertake an in-house Frontline Problem-Solving Root Cause Analysis Development Program typically involving a one-day workshop or two half-day workshops for say 3–4 teams of 4–5 people followed by weekly 1–2 hour team meetings for each team. At these meetings, teams progressively work through at least three recent problems or incidents from their workplace, resulting in bottom-line gains as your people learn and apply Frontline Problem-Solving Root Cause Analysis.

By initially working in a team of 4–5 people, the learning process can be accelerated so that after completing the three problems to the agreed standard, each team member should be able to tackle a problem by themselves with the support of a trained in-house facilitator.

Ideally, the program should not exceed 12 weeks; however, depending on the experience of the participants and the difficulty of the frontline problems selected, the timeframe can be reduced. Figure 6.4 provides an example of an 8-week program we conducted for an organisation wanting to train 15 people in 3 teams of 5.

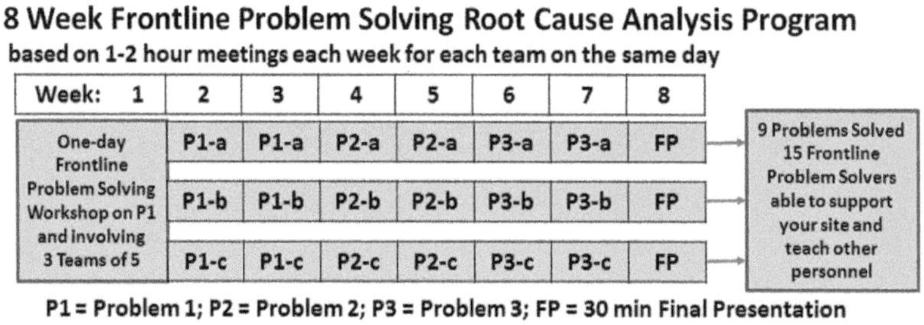

8 Week Frontline Problem Solving Root Cause Analysis Program
based on 1-2 hour meetings each week for each team on the same day

Week:	1	2	3	4	5	6	7	8	
One-day Frontline Problem Solving Workshop on P1 and involving 3 Teams of 5		P1-a	P1-a	P2-a	P2-a	P3-a	P3-a	FP	9 Problems Solved 15 Frontline Problem Solvers able to support your site and teach other personnel
		P1-b	P1-b	P2-b	P2-b	P3-b	P3-b	FP	
		P1-c	P1-c	P2-c	P2-c	P3-c	P3-c	FP	

P1 = Problem 1; P2 = Problem 2; P3 = Problem 3; FP = 30 min Final Presentation

Figure 6.4   **Example 8 week Frontline Problem-Solving Root Cause Analysis program.**

10 Week Frontline Problem Solving Root Cause Analysis Program
based on 1-2 hour meetings each week for each team on the same day

Weeks: 1&2	3	4	5	6	7	8	9	10	
One-day Frontline Problem Solving Workshop (spread over 2 half days) focused on P1 and involving 4 Teams of 5	P1-a	P1-a	P2-a	P2-a	P2-a	P3-a	P3-a	FP	12 Problems Solved 20 Frontline Problem Solvers able to support your site and teach other personnel
	P1-b	P1-b	P2-b	P2-b	P2-b	P3-b	P3-b	FP	
	P1-c	P1-c	P2-c	P2-c	P2-c	P3-c	P3-c	FP	
	P1-d	P1-d	P2-d	P2-d	P2-d	P3-d	P3-d	FP	

P1 = Problem 1; P2 = Problem 2; P3 = Problem 3; FP = 30 min Final Presentation

Figure 6.5   **Example 10 week Frontline Problem-Solving Root Cause Analysis program.**

Another model used by some organisations is to break the one-day workshop into 2 half-day workshops, extend the program and have four teams involved rather than three (Figure 6.5).

Some of the tools used to support the teams as they develop their problem-solving skills are a comprehensive Workshop Manual, three coloured user workbooks (one for each problem), a soft copy of the Frontline Problem-Solving Root Cause Analysis A3 Summary Sheet and for each team a set of A0- sized laminated wall charts covering Cause & Effect Diagram, Why-Why Diagram and the Frontline Problem-Solving Root Cause Analysis A3 Summary Sheet (Figure 6.6).

Identifying the Initial Frontline Problems for Your Development Program

Each team (typically 3 or 4 teams of 4–5 employees per workshop with each team having a designated Leader for each problem) is required to provide at least one recent incident type problem (ideally three to allow the team to select the one they feel most comfortable addressing) for their team to work through during the workshop.

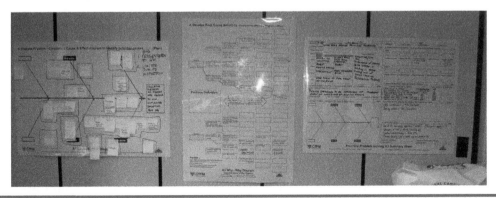

Figure 6.6   **A0 size laminated Cause & Effect Diagram, Why-Why diagram and A3 Summary Sheet.**

An incident type problem as defined earlier in this chapter, is an event that occurs that stops the shift from achieving one of its performance expectations, For example quality expectation down due to a pallet of rework or scrap, or output below expectation due to a breakdown.

It is important to select recent incident type problems that your team will be reasonably familiar with to allow the team to explore all of the possible reasons for their selected incident type problem. Hence the **date and time of the incident** (when problem occurred and was discovered) should be clear to everyone.

Typical questions your nominated leader of each team could ask and address before coming to the workshop are:

- Have you found a measure that shows the deviation from expectation clearly?
- Have you got a process map or picture along with supporting data that makes it easier for everyone to understand the problem?
- Can you define the gap between current performance and target or expected performance?
- Can you identify the possible impact on the business if the problem is solved?
- Can you identify where the problem was initiated from?
- Have you got any history relating to similar problems?

The selected list of possible incident-type problems for the workshop should be discussed with the person who is presenting well before the workshop in case further scoping of the problem or more information is required.

To assist in selecting suitable incident-type problems, we include a few fictitious but typical examples:

- Carton erector jams increased from 2 per shift to 10 per shift last night
- The conveyor to the primary mixer trips at random throughout the shift for no apparent reason
- The primary crusher keeps intermittently tripping during the shift
- Product waste increased from the usual 2% to over 5% yesterday
- The lube tank overflowed for no apparent reason on afternoon shift causing lost production and a lot of frustration for operators who had to clean up
- Line 2 had a 10% increase in rejects on Wednesday nightshift
- Conveyor number 4 has been tripping every half hour for the past two shifts
- The clutch assembly line has had a reduced output rate from 32 to 27 per hour for the past 24 hours
- The bag filler has been stopping intermittently for no apparent reason for most of yesterday
- The first batch produced this morning had a higher number of failures than for the rest of the day
- The product labels kept moving out of position during the run yesterday

- The kiln temperature has been unstable for the past 24 hours
- All products from heat treatment plant number 1 failed the hardness test during afternoon shift and now need to be reworked
- Half of yesterday's production was underweight and has been rejected by the Quality Department

Finding the Resources for On-Going Frontline Problem-Solving Root Cause Analysis

The challenge for most organisations is how best to allocate limited resources to the required amount of Frontline Problem-Solving Root Cause Analysis.

An effective way to manage limited resources is to establish improvement policies that limit the amount of time allocated for Frontline Problem-Solving Root Cause Analysis. A problem or incident needs to have caused an agreed impact on performance before being allocated. For example, triggers are set and when exceeded, a person will be allocated to take responsibility for the Frontline Problem-Solving Root Cause Analysis process and report back within an agreed number of working days with proposed root cause solutions and an action plan for approval. Basically, the nominated person would play detective, visit the scene of the incident and question appropriate people to define the problem, ensure proper containment if required, then engage the appropriate people to assist in developing the Cause & Effect Diagram and the Why-Why Diagram.

The typical policy for initially regulating the workload could be that a person can only be allocated to determine and have approved the action plan for one Frontline Problem-Solving Root Cause Analysis at a time, and that they have three (3) working days to report back the proposed action plan. Obviously once the action plan is agreed, then realistic target dates can be set for the completion and final report back.

The triggers should cover the 'cause' Key Success Factors discussed in Chapter 3 – Element 3: Appropriate Measures, and be progressively refined as fewer problems or incidents occur. For example, Toyota initiates a Frontline Problem-Solving Root Cause Analysis activity if they have a breakdown on their assembly line of *'greater than 2 minutes'*, whereas most organisations not advanced on their improvement journey may make their starting trigger as *'greater than 1 hour'* or in some cases *'greater than 2 hours'*. The key is to set triggers then regularly review them and tighten them as performance of your people and the plant improves from the successful Frontline Problem-Solving Root Cause Analysis activities. For example, you may do a 3-month review and re-adjust the triggers by reducing them by say 10% so that after 18 months you would have halved the trigger.

Some companies also allocate time each day for the work personnel assigned to a Frontline Problem-Solving Root Cause Analysis to have access to a competent in-house facilitator who can assist them if required; for example, at 1.00 pm each day for half-an-hour the facilitator is available in a training room with white-board to assist with the process or documenting the outcomes on a Frontline Problem-Solving Root Cause Analysis A3 Summary Sheet.

Outline of the 7 Step Frontline Problem-Solving Root Cause Analysis Process

The Frontline Problem-Solving Root Cause Analysis involves 7 steps including Cause & Effect Analysis supported by a Cause & Effect Diagram, and Why-Why Analysis supported by a Why-Why Diagram.

To demonstrate the 7-step process a case study will be used throughout as we explain each step.

CASE STUDY – BROKEN CLASSIC PAVERS

The plant manufactures a range of cement blocks and pavers. It has two production lines – Line 1 and Line 2; both lines are designed to be the same. Its three main paver products are the Classic, Regular and Special which all come in a range of colours. All three pavers are made by the same process and have the same material mix and can be made on either line. The difference in the pavers is their size, all three pavers are the same thickness (35 mm), the Classic paver is 200×200 mm, the Regular paver is 180×180 mm and the Special paver is 150×150 mm.

The process for making all the pavers is the same, only the mould changes. The raw materials are carefully weighed into a batch mixing unit. The raw materials are sand, aggregate, recycled crushed block (if uncoloured), colour (in the form of oxide) and cement.

The raw materials are mixed dry and a small amount of process water is added. The amount of water is critical as too much water will make the mixture too sloppy and the blocks will not form, not enough water and the blocks will crumble after curing.

The mix is fed in controlled amounts into the press. The press contains a mould sitting on a steel plate. The mix is fed into the mould and then pressed and vibrated for a controlled time. After a short period, the mould is lifted off the plate and this leaves the pavers standing on their narrow sides in two rows of 15 pavers on the steel plate. This is a great improvement from 6 months ago where a process improvement team increased the pavers per mould from 24 to 30, (2 rows of 12 pavers to 2 rows of 15). The old mould was much narrower than the current mould and there was a lot of unused space on the steel plate. The potential difficulty with this is the pavers are now made very close to the edge (refer to Figure 6.7) if the plates are not cleaned properly or there is some corrosion on the plate a slight vibration can knock the pavers over (refer to Figures 6.8 and 6.9).

Figure 6.7 **A full plate of pavers.**

Figure 6.8 **Edge pavers falling off top row.**

Figure 6.9 **Toppling pavers.**

The wet pavers are carried by a conveyor belt to the loader. At the loader each tray is automatically lifted off the conveyor and put in a rack which is on rails. Each rack will hold four trays per slide and there are five slides per rack. The racks are attached to bogies or mini rail cars that transport the un-cured pavers into the kiln for curing. The kiln is a closed off area where steam is injected under low pressure to maintain the temperature at 55°C and 100% humidity. The trays are pulled around the kiln for 4 hours while the pavers cure and harden off.

At the end of the kiln the racks arrive at the stripping machine. The stripping machine performs two functions, the first is to unload the trays off the rack and secondly, place them on a conveyor. A short distance down the conveyor the pavers are stripped off the steel tray by a pair of hydraulically controlled pads and placed on a conveyor to the turner. The turner, also modified by the improvement team, now picks up 15 pavers at a time and turns them 90 degrees so that they sit on the large surface and not end on. The pavers are then transported by the conveyor to the automatic packers where the pavers are again lifted by hydraulic pads and placed on to wooden pallets ready for wrapping and delivery to the despatch area.

OTHER INFORMATION

30 pavers are made each press cycle and a cycle takes 30 seconds, therefore 60 pavers are made per minute or 3,600 per hour. Each rack has four trays per slide, and there are five slides per rack, so each rack holds 600 pavers. At this rate $3,600/600 = 6$ racks per hour. Racks are in the kiln for 4 hours so the number of racks in a kiln $= 6 \times 4 = 24$.

CURRENT OPERATION

The plant is run 24 hours a day 5 days a week with two days per week set aside for maintenance or additional production if required. The plant is run with three shift operators, the first operator is responsible for the feed end of both lines and the second operator is responsible for the kiln discharge area to the packers where their main function is to remove any broken pavers and throw them in the reject skip. The third operator is the Leading Hand who is responsible for ensuring the production plan for both lines is met and provide additional assistance as required.

With pressure from the marketplace to lower the cost of the pavers in order to remain competitive, the company has embarked on a productivity initiative involving the Research and Development Department to see if the press vibrating time can be reduced and the kiln speed increased to increase capacity and hence lower unit cost. As such, trials have been progressing for the past 4 weeks where there has been 2.0% incremental change each week then monitoring the output.

THE INCIDENT

At the nightshift hand-over meeting to dayshift, it was reported that just over 4 hours ago a rack of Classic pavers emerged from Line 1 kiln with most of the pavers broken – only about 100 could be recovered. By the time the nightshift Leading Hand got to the packing area everything was running as expected, he hung around for twenty minutes and watched two racks emerge, but there was no repeat of this event and all production looked good. The broken pavers were cleared up and placed in the waste skips.

About an hour into the dayshift the operator from the packing area on Line 1 calls on the radio to say a rack of Classic pavers have arrived mostly broken at the packing station. The Frontline Leader orders Line 1 to stop and for all the broken pavers to be cleared up. Again about 100 were recovered. While this is happening the Frontline Leader takes the opportunity to walk around Line 1 to see if there are any other clues to what has happened. Everything appears to be normal. There are no broken pavers at the press or the loader. There are no signs of any broken pavers at the entrance to the kiln. The line is restarted and initially there is no repeat of the incident. All the finished pavers on the racks coming out of Line 1 kiln are fine and there are good pavers at the stripper.

About an hour later The Frontline Leader attend the Production Managers Daily Review Meeting and reports the two incidents. As the quality loss was much greater than the current Root Cause Analysis (RCA) trigger for any rack incident, The Frontline Leader is asked to conduct a Frontline Problem-Solving Root Cause Analysis and report back to the meeting within three days as to what needs to be done so this problem never occurs again.

Step 1: Define the Problem

Once the problem can be defined in simple, easy to understand terms, it is much easier to solve and to communicate to other people. Spending the time up front is never wasted as this is often the most difficult step to master as in many cases people get confused between a problem and a situation.

For a problem to exist and be identifiable it needs to meet three criteria:

1. Performance is different from expectation;
2. The reason for the difference is not known; and
3. The reason for the difference needs to be known before expectation can be achieve or the problem is stopped from happening again.

If your answer is YES to all three statements, then you have a frontline problem. It is also worth noting, poorly defined expectations will lead to poorly defined problems. This is why setting very clear targets or expectations as out-lined in Chapter 5 is critical before embarking on Frontline Problem-Solving Root Cause Analysis.

There are nine actions which should be completed when defining a frontline problem:

Step #	Action
1.1	Establish an **object-deviation** Problem Statement
1.2	Describe **what** the problem is and is not
1.3	Describe **where** the problem is and is not
1.4	Describe **when** the problem Iis and is not
1.5	Describe the **size** of the problem clearly
1.6	Identify the **Point of Observation** of the problem
1.7	Identify the **Point of Occurrence** of the problem
1.8	Define the **deviation** between the current performance and expected performance using appropriate supporting material
1.9	Document the series of events leading up to the problem along with any **history** of previous or similar problems

EFFECTIVE QUESTIONING

A key skill we need to master to be an effective frontline problem solver is the ability to conduct effective **questioning.**

Effective questioning is**:**

■ The way we gain information;
■ How we can confirm or deny information; and
■ How we can engage people to assist in identifying and solving the problem

There are three types of questions that are important in frontline problem solving:

Open Questions: Invite long or unrestricted answers with the aim to gather or understand new information. They usually start with What, Where, When, How, Who or Why, and they cannot be answered with a Yes or No.

Closed Questions: Imply the answer so as to check and/or confirm answers. They usually start with Do, Have, Will, Can, Are or Is, and they can be answered with a Yes or No.

Questioning to the Void: Seeking out a more specific answer so as to gather better or clearer information. They usually involve re-asking the question based on the previous answer, however also asking 'what else'. The void is when you stop making progress.

When defining a frontline problem, we find it helpful to first start with a *Problem Statement*, then expand with a *Problem Description,* then combine both to create a *Problem Definition*.

Problem Statement:

How do we know that the expectation is not being achieved, or what is happening that we did not expect?

1.1 Establish Problem Statement in Object-Deviation Format

- What thing (process, equipment, material etc.) is not doing what we expect (**object**)?
- What performance has changed (**deviation**)?
- How do we know the thing is not doing what we expect?

Before creating a Problem Statement go and see; collect data; take photos; talk to those involved – ***then*** write a short statement in **object-deviation** format. By using a standard format it becomes easier for everyone to read and understand your A3 Summary Sheet. For example:

- Line 1 Kiln – produced broken Classic pavers
- Pump 3 – has low flow
- Raw material – has low viscosity

Problem Description:

How to describe what is wrong factually so as to increase our understanding of the problem. It involves looking at five dimensions: What, Where, When, Size and Point of Occurrence. As we look at each dimension we need to ask: What data do we have to support this?

1.2 What Is the Problem?

- What is the thing we are having the problem with?
- What is wrong with it?

1.3 Where Did We Find the Problem? (Point of Observation)

- Where on the thing (the object) is what's wrong with it? (the deviation)
- Where is the thing when it goes wrong? (geographic location)

1.4 When Did It Happen?

- When did we first notice the problem?
- When since then has the problem occurred? Is there any pattern?
- When in the life of the process or cycle has the problem occurred?

For each of the 'what', 'where' and 'when' questions, there is a second question we can ask:-

Not only 'What **IS** the problem' but 'What **IS NOT** the problem'. For example, at a site making a range of pavers for the building industry, the questioning could be:

- What **is** the problem? Answer: Classic pavers.
- What **is not** the problem? Answer: Regular or Special pavers.

This hopefully gives us something to compare with.

1.5 Size or Measure of the Deviation from Standard or Extent of the Problem

- How much product or output was affected?
- How many quality parameters are affected?
- What are the tangible and intangible impacts on safety, quality, delivery, equipment and people?
- What is this costing the site?

1.6 Point of Observation or Where Did You First Identify You Had a Problem

Often the Point of Observation is not where the problem is originating especially if it is the exit point of a process as in the case study where the broken pavers were seen at the exit of the kiln. However, it becomes obvious that the problem was either in the kiln or before the kiln.

1.7 Point of Occurrence or Where Do You Believe the Problem Is Originating From

Before a problem can be solved to root cause, the problem's Point of Occurrence **MUST** be identified. Sometimes the Point of Occurrence or Point of Observation is not where the problem is identified or Point of Observation. For example: underweight of product could be identified at weight scales which is the Point of Observation, however the Point of Occurrence could be at the filling machine. Try and find the Point of Occurrence by 'go and see'. Also, at this point it may be helpful to create a High Level Process Flow Map or Diagram to ensure there is a clear understanding of the entire situation.

If you have difficulties identifying the Point of Occurrence, it may be because you have a broad or vague problem. The key challenge is to spend the time to actually identify the Point of Occurrence before trying to solve the perceived problem or, your problem may be a combination of problems.

CHALLENGE OF IDENTIFYING THE PROBLEM

At one of our Frontline Problem-Solving Root Cause Analysis public workshops a team bought along a problem of excessive lost time due to a crane bearing failure. When we started to delve into the problem, it came out that the lost time was not only caused by the failure of the bearing, but also by the time delay before the failure was identified. In their situation, the crane was remotely controlled from the control room and the bearing had failed some days earlier and nobody realised it. When it was finally identified the bearing had welded itself to the shaft so it took extended time to carry out the repair. So, we really had two problems: why did the bearing fail, and why did it take so long to identify the failure?

Possible consequences of not identifying the Point of Occurrence as part of the Problem Definition:

■ Lack of consensus or buy-in on what to do to solve the problem (different perceptions of what the Point of Occurrence really is)
■ Fixing and addressing symptoms rather than the root cause resulting in recurrence of the problem after it has been 'solved'

1.8 Problem Definition = Problem Statement + Problem Description

A clear and agreed Problem Definition is crucial in really understanding the problem or incident you are trying to address. It should consist of the following three elements:

1. Clear identification of the Point of Occurrence e.g.: Line 1 kiln
2. Clear definition of the problem variable e.g.: broken Classic pavers
3. Clear identification of the magnitude of the problem e.g.: 80% of two racks (Figure 6.10)

When presenting your Problem Definition you may find it helpful to verify it with supporting material you gathered during your investigation such as the Process Flow Map or diagram outlining the process and highlighting the Point of Observation and Point of Occurrence, incident reports and photographs (Figure 6.11).

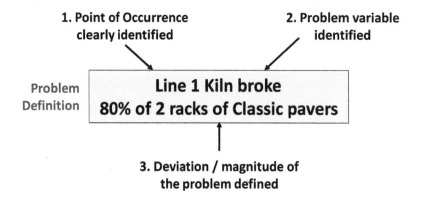

Figure 6.10 **Constructing a problem definition.**

1.9 Problem History or the Sequence of Events Leading Up to the Problem

- What issues or events occurred prior to the problem being identified?
- Has this problem or a similar problem occurred before?
- Has this problem or a similar problem occurred in other areas?
- Was a Frontline Problem-Solving Root Cause Analysis A3 Summary Sheet previously developed to solve a similar problem?

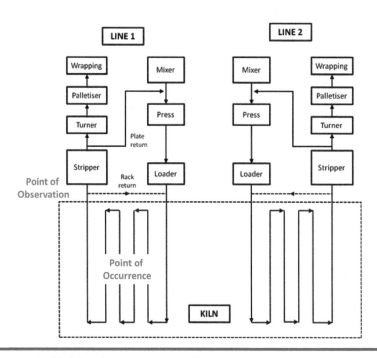

Figure 6.11 **Example high level process flow diagram.**

1. Define Problem (Plan)

Problem Statement: Line 1 Kiln produced broken Classic pavers			

Problem Description:

	Is	**Is Not**	**Problem Definition**
What	Classic Pavers	Regular or Special Pavers	Line 1 Kiln broke 80% of 2 racks of Classic pavers
	Broken	Cracked, wrong colour, not cured	
Where	All over the Paver	In one place only	
	On Line 1	On Line 2	**Cost to Business**
	At the exit of the Kiln	At the entrance to the Kiln	Each Classic paver costs $1.80 to make, approx 24c to clear up when broken and 4c to dump the waste. Cost of 1000 Classic pavers is $2,080
When	During 2 batches of Classic pavers	During batches of Regular or Special pavers	
	During Nightshift and Dayshift	During Afternoon shift	Add to this the need to reschedule production time to make an additional 1000 plus Classic pavers of that colour.
	In the Kiln during curing	Before the Kiln after the stripper	
Size	2 rack of about 500 pavers out of 600 per rack (1000 pavers)		
	>80% of batch compared to standard of > 2.5%		
	Will impact deliver as will have to replace the 1000 pavers		
	$2,080 in material loss, clean up, disposal plus lost production		
Point of Observation	Exit of Kiln on Line 1		
Point of Occurrence	Inside Line 1 Kiln		

Problem History – No history of previous similar problems. R&D Trials been progressing for 4 weeks on press vibration time and Kiln speed (2% change each week)

Figure 6.12   Case study Step 1 define problem.

■ Is there any history of any changes or work done at or near the Point of Occurrence of the problem? (Figure 6.12)

Step 2: Contain Problem

Often containment is needed straight away to stop the problem from getting any bigger or to make the area safe. As such it is important to determine if anything needs to be done in the short term to get the problem under control until you can identify and eliminate the root cause(s).

The aim is to reduce the risk of on-going adverse impacts from the problem. If the problem is not contained, there is a risk that it may reoccur with subsequent loss. It also provides an opportunity to prove that the Point of Occurrence has been identified because often the containment action has to be applied at the Point of Occurrence. As such, the successful application of the containment action may indicate that you have correctly identified the Point of Occurrence.

Containment actions should be immediately implemented and easy to monitor. Examples of possible actions include:

■ Fix the breakdown and increase monitoring on the equipment
■ Put the rejects into a separate bin so that you can clearly see them
■ Set up regular performance monitoring to ensure that things are kept on track
■ Barricade off the area to prevent access
■ Instruct people to use Personal Protective Equipment (PPE)

There are four actions which should be completed when containing the problem:

Step#	Action
2.1	Identify a containment action if required
2.2	Enact a containment action if required
2.3	Communicate the containment action to everyone involved with the process to ensure containment is maintained
2.4	Incorporate monitoring of containment action in the Daily Review Process to ensure containment is sufficient to address the short-term issues

2.1 Identify a Containment Action

Use the hierarchy of controls to help determine the most appropriate action starting with the highest level to gain the most effective short-term control over the situation. If you cannot implement or sustain a control at a higher level, then consider a lower level of control.

For example: 'we still need to use the chemical while we investigate alternatives, so ensure that there is effective personal protective equipment available and that everyone is properly instructed in its use'.

If the lower level control is ineffective, then consider a higher level of control. For example: 'roping off the equipment is not effective so we need to shut down until the guard is updated'.

Consider using appropriate in-house risk assessment processes to determine the effectiveness of various options (Figure 6.13).

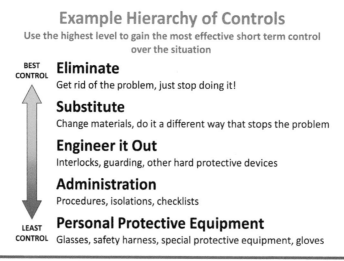

Figure 6.13   **Example hierarchy of controls.**

2.2 Enact the Containment Action

Once selected, develop an Implementation Plan for the containment action (quick fix) which identifies:

■ Instructions on how to implement the containment action;
■ Person or persons responsible to undertake the instructions; and
■ Date and place the containment action will be put into place.

2.3 Communicate the Containment Action

Determine who needs to be informed regarding the short-term containment action (quick fix), and what is expected of them. Ideally a record should be kept of who is spoken to (all employees involved with the process), what is conveyed (change of practice, expected timeframe until problem solved) and how it is conveyed (toolbox meeting, special briefing, individually) including date and time.

2.4 Verify the Effectiveness of the Containment Action

If you implement a containment action, ensure appropriate follow-up and support so that it is effective. Establish follow-up checks at specific dates and times where you specify what is to be checked and ensure the effectiveness of the containment is monitored during the appropriate Daily Review Meeting (Figure 6.14).

> *Ensure you go and have a look at the containment yourself. Make sure it is working effectively before moving on.*

Step 3: Analyse Problem

Determine what could have caused the problem to occur by conducting a Cause & Effect Analysis using a Cause & Effect Diagram supported by any other appropriate problem-solving tools to explore the possible variables or issues why the frontline problem exists.

2. Contain Problem – Detail the containment action required and completed			(Plan)
Detail the containment action that has been taken:			
At the time we cleaned up all the broken pavers to make the area safe. All shifts have been advised to monitor the situation until we carry out a full maintenance inspection of the Kiln including all Racks, Bogies, Wheels and Rails, and we complete the RCA.			
Date Implemented:	Place Implemented:	Implemented by:	Verification of action by:
10 June	At Kiln 1	Production Supervisor	Production Manager

Figure 6.14   Case study Step 2 contain problem.

A Cause & Effect Analysis is a structured brainstorming process to assist you to:

■ Gain further insight into the problem;
■ Identify all possible variables or issues impacting on the effect of the problem;
■ Categorise and group the variables or issues;
■ Review the variables or issues to determine which ones to follow up with.

A Cause & Effect Diagram consists of a number of parts:

■ **Effect Statement** (same or similar to Problem Definition)
  – Clearly defines what the problem effect is and what you are investigating.
■ **Categories** (standard 4 four are People, Machine, Methods, Materials)
  – Promote brainstorming, however use categories that are meaningful to your problem.
■ **Brainstormed possible causes** (variables or issues) that relate back to the Effect Statement and are sufficiently specific and focussed preferably written in **object-deviation** format
  – Placed on the diagram linked to the appropriate category (Figure 6.15).

There are nine actions which should be completed when conducting a Cause & Effect Analysis using a Cause & Effect Diagram. These nine actions can be further subdivided into Preparation, Construction and Prioritisation:

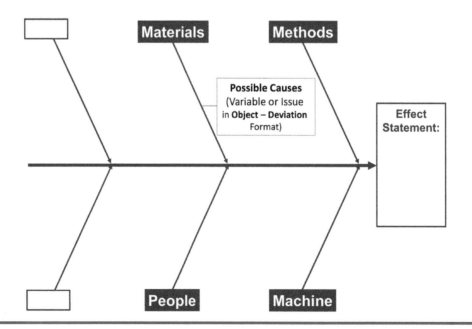

Figure 6.15 **Example cause and effect diagram.**

	Step #	Actions
Preparation	3.1	Confirm the Effect Statement
	3.2	Identify those to be involved
	3.3	Identify questions and information required
	3.4	Prepare materials
Construction	3.5	Select the initial categories to promote the brainstorming
	3.6	Populate the Cause & Effect Diagram
	3.7	Conduct quality check of the possible causes
Prioritisation	3.8	Eliminate or confirm possible causes
	3.9	Select most significant possible causes

3.1 Confirm the Effect Statement

A clear and agreed Effect Statement is crucial for completing a Cause & Effect Diagram. Like the Problem Definition created in Step 1, it should have the following three elements:

1. Clear identification of the Point of Occurrence – e.g.: Line 1 kiln;
2. Clear definition of the problem variable or issue – e.g.: broke;
3. Clear identification of the magnitude of the problem – e.g.: 80% of two racks of Classic pavers.

   Effect Statement: Line 1 kiln broke 80% of two racks of Classic pavers

3.2 Identify Those to Be Involved

Formal brainstorming sessions should be limited to 4–8 people at a time, hopefully with a spread of people who can look at the problem from different perspectives. Sometimes several sessions can be helpful to allow people to walk away and reflect for a while. Alternatively, if multi-shifts are involved then having each shift contribute can be beneficial especially to share the learning and feel part of the solution. As such, thought should also be given to determine the most appropriate time and place for the brainstorming and whether an A0-sized laminated Cause & Effect Diagram will be used so that it is easy for everyone to contribute, and if so where is the best place to locate it.

3.3 Identify Questions and Information Required

When bringing a group together to brainstorm all the possible causes (variables or issues) it can be helpful to prepare relevant background information to help people understand the breadth of the problem. This is where the information collected during Steps 1 and 2 can be very helpful, especially the High-Level Process Flow Map created to support your Problem Definition. A range of prompting questions should also be pre-arranged such as:

- Is the process simple, straightforward and understood?
- What do our observations of the workplace identify?
- Is there a standard operating procedure or work procedure for this activity?
- Does it address the problem?
- Does everyone follow it?

3.4 Prepare Materials

When preparing to construct the Cause & Effect Diagram we have found it helpful to have:

- Post-it notes to capture and then sort the ideas;
- Markers for everyone to write on the post-it notes;
- A0-sized laminated Cause & Effect Diagram to ensure sufficient space to place the post-it notes; and
- Digital camera to record the results.

3.5 Select the Initial Categories to Promote the Brainstorming

If equipment focused then People, Machine, Method, Materials may be a good start whereas if process focused then Systems or Information may be more appropriate than Machine. Other options could include Environment or Time. The key is to select categories that are meaningful to the problem that can be used to prompt the brainstorming. Some people like to randomly brainstorm all possible causes to the problem (Effect Statement) then group under the categories, while an alternative approach is to use each category to promote more focused brainstorming. In other words, if Method is one of your categories, everyone would focus on all the Method's variables or issues that could cause or impact on the problem (Effect Statement). Then once that is exhausted, move onto the next category recognising there will always be some back tracking or new thoughts regarding a previous category brought about by working on another category.

3.6 Populate the Cause & Effect Diagram

- Write in the Effect Statement at the righthand end of the Cause & Effect Diagram in the box provided
- Write in agreed major categories
- For each category, brainstorm all the possible causes (variables or issues) that could cause the effect then clearly write each one onto a post-it note or

similar using **object-deviation** format so they are easy to read and understand, and accurately reflect the cause
■ Organise the notes onto the main category stems
■ Duplicate notes if they belong in more than one category stem
■ Consolidate notes if similar and in same category stem
■ Tidy up diagram by removing notes and writing in agreed causes using **object-deviation** format
■ Draw in the appropriate lines and nodes to make groups
■ Use consensus to complete
■ Highlight areas of further investigation or analysis

3.7 Conduct Quality Check of the Causes

The Cause & Effect Diagram should be carefully quality checked at this point by checking the spread of causes on the diagram:

■ Are the causes well distributed across the diagram or are they clustered into a single category or grouping?
■ If they are clustered, is this justified or is it a reflection of specific bias by the people constructing the diagram?
■ Do we need to seek further input or clarification from others?
■ Does the diagram accurately reflect the breadth and the depth of the problem?

Finally, check the linkage between individual causes and the effect:

■ Are the causes well worded? Are they clear and specific and potentially actionable for further investigation? Can you say 'If < cause > then < effect >'?
■ Do the causes provide further insight into the problem or do they just 'muddy the water'? Causes should help to provide further detail and focus.
■ Beware of vague or poorly defined causes such as 'training poor'. In what way specifically has this contributed to the effect? Ask for explanations and clarification?
■ Rewrite causes if required.
■ Ensure evidence is there to support the relationship between the cause and the effect?

3.8 Eliminate or Confirm Causes

A Cause & Effect Diagram is only useful if it helps to prioritise areas for action based on facts (causes supported by evidence) rather than fiction (causes without evidence). As such evidence is needed to link the various causes to the effect.

■ What data or evidence is required to either eliminate or confirm the causes?
■ Are these causes able to be resolved by yourself or do you need to seek assistance from others such as external suppliers, engineers or quality technicians to eliminate or confirm causes?

Test and verify each cause through examining history documents and collecting relevant evidence.

THE FOUR TYPES OF EVIDENCE YOU MAY COME ACROSS

Sensed Evidence – **direct observation (sight, sound, smell, touch, taste)**

- This uses the individuals senses directly;
- Different people would sense the same thing;
- High emphasis is placed upon 'go and see' – use your senses.

Inferred Evidence – **deduced from cause & effect relationships**
- An outcome inferred from personal experience or an established cause & effect relationship, for example a smile on someone's face leads to belief that they are happy.

Intuition Based Evidence – **experience**
- Occurs at subconscious level – not capable of explaining origin, for example a high injury rate may lead people to intuit that people do not know how to work safely.

Emotional Based Evidence – **feelings**
- Emotions and feelings exist in the limbic system within the old reptilian portion of the brain while senses and reasoning exist in the cortex part of the brain; hence, someone with strong feelings may have difficulty seeing the reasoning as they are not well connected.

The quality of evidence is greater if it is sensed rather than emotional based. Sometimes it can be difficult to progress if people feel strongly about a specific issue (using emotional-based evidence). Rather than ignoring outright, it may be worthwhile to explore how the emotional 'I feel it is so' can be changed into 'sensed evidence' through observation, audits, or measurement, recognising that emotions and feelings exist in a different part of the brain than senses and reasoning, and often people with strong feelings need to experience the evidence by going and seeing for themselves.

3.9 Select the Most Significant Possible Causes

After all the remaining causes have been validated by evidence and their potential impact is understood, a few or most often two causes will stand out as the main contributors to the effect. Highlight the two most significant causes you

3. Analyse Problem – Summary Cause & Effect Diagram showing Significant Causes   (Plan)

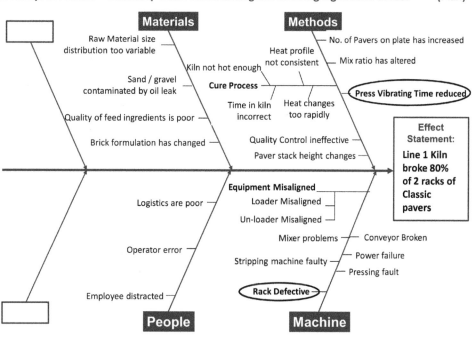

Figure 6.16   Case study Step 3 summary Cause & Effect Diagram showing significant causes.

need to investigate with Why-Why Analysis on the assumption that by fixing these causes we will fix the problem. If this is not true, then review analysis to date.

■ Use data to verify the validity of the perceived significant causes
■ Challenge people's perceptions by providing evidence
■ Check validity in the workplace by going and seeing before progressing

Key pitfall – selecting causes for further investigation based on gut feel rather than using reliable data as evidence (Figure 6.16).

Step 4: Develop Root Cause Solutions

Now that we have identified what we believe to be the two main causes using our Cause & Effect Diagram, we now need to dig beneath these symptoms and get to the underlying or root causes using Why-Why Analysis.

It is not a single sharply defined process as it is based on asking 'why' many times with the aid of a Why-Why Diagram to capture the various answers in a structured way. The Why-Why Diagram or 5 Whys Diagram is one of the most common and effective tools to assist in finding the possible root causes to a problem to ensure that the problem is fixed once and for all, provided the answers to each 'why' are supported and verified with data or observational evidence.

We also find at this point as you explore the 'whys' you sometimes have to go back and redefine the problem you are looking at. For example one team we were working with had as their problem 'Filling machine has inconsistent counting resulting in 25% of batch reworked'. During the Cause & Effect Analysis one of the main causes was 'vision counter faulty'. When asking why, during the Why-Why Analysis it was identified that the glass cover on the vision counter had a crack in it. When asking why again it become obvious if this was the problem then we could use a Cause & Effect Diagram to look at all the many reasons for the glass to get cracked rather than limiting the discussion to the space available on the Why-Why Diagram.

This is why we say 'Why-Why Analysis is not a sharply defined process' and as such it is why having an experienced facilitator is very important to support your people as they develop their experience (Figure 6.17).

There are 10 actions which should be completed when conducting a Why-Why Analysis using a Why-Why Diagram so as to develop root cause solutions. These 10 actions can be further subdivided into Preparation, Construction and Drive to Action:

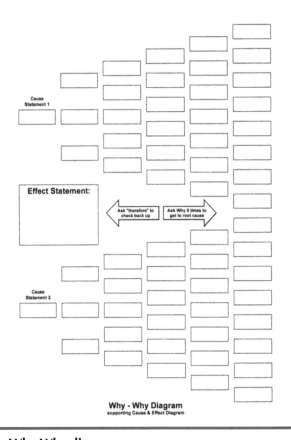

Figure 6.17   Example Why-Why diagram.

	Step #	Actions
Preparation	4.1	Extend main causes into cause statements
	4.2	Identify those to be involved
	4.3	Identify questions and Information required
	4.4	Prepare materials
Construction	4.5	Enter Cause Statements and populate the Why-Why Diagram
	4.6	Verify each answer to a Why with data or observational evidence
	4.7	Summarise the root cause pathways that will best address the problem (Effect Statement)
Drive to Action	4.8	Identify possible solution or solutions to each cause in the two pathways
	4.9	Select all the solutions you can work on
	4.10	Select all the remaining solutions you can recommend to others

Before you run a session to conduct the Why-Why Analysis you will need to do some preparatory work.

4.1 Extend Main Causes into Cause Statements

Extend the two causes highlighted on your Cause & Effect Diagram by adding the magnitude of the cause to create a Cause Statement that is as clear and specific as possible. The following three elements are recommended for a good Cause Statement:

1. Clear identification of the *object* impacted (where the solution needs to be applied) – e.g.: press vibrating time;
2. Clear definition of the *deviation* from the standard – e.g.: reduced;
3. Clear identification of the *magnitude* of the problem – e.g.: by 8%.

   Cause Statement: Press vibrating time reduced by 8% – mix may not be compacted enough.

4.2 Identify Those to Be Involved

Why-Why Analysis brainstorming sessions to generate the Why-Why Diagram should be limited to 4–8 people at a time, hopefully with a spread of people who can look at the causes from different perspectives. Sometimes several sessions can be helpful to allow people to walk away and reflect for a while. Alternatively, if multi-shifts are involved then having each shift contribute can be beneficial especially to share the learning and feel part of the solution. As such, thought should also be given to determine the most appropriate time and place for the Why-Why Analysis sessions and whether an A0-sized laminated Why-Why Diagram will be used so that it is easy for everyone to contribute, and if so where is the best place to locate it.

4.3 Identify Questions and Information Required

When bringing a group together to conduct a Why-Why Analysis brainstorm session, it can be helpful to prepare relevant background information to help people understand the breadth of the problem. This is where the information collected during Steps 1, 2 and 3 can be very helpful, especially the Cause & Effect Diagram created to identify the main causes being addressed. Other questions to consider are:

- Who will collect data to support each step of the Why-Why Analysis?
- When will you go out into the workplace to check and see what is happening?

4.4 Prepare Materials

When preparing to construct the Why-Why Diagram we have found it helpful to have:

1. Post-it notes to capture the answers to the Why questions;
2. Markers for everyone to write on the post-it notes;
3. A0-sized laminated Why-Why Diagram to ensure sufficient space to place the post-it notes; and
4. Digital camera to record the results.

4.5 Enter Cause Statements and Populate the Why-Why Diagram

For each Cause, ask 'why did this cause occur' or alternatively 'what caused this' and brainstorm possible reasons why. Check logic by working back using 'therefore'. This is a useful trick to confirm that you have identified the correct issue. It is vital that the focus is kept narrow by watching out for ballooning issues such as 'training', or 'management', or 'maintenance'.

Where ever possible we suggest using object-deviation format (noun–verb combinations) and writing each answer onto a post-it note and placing it onto the Why-Why Diagram.

For each why, ask 'why' again and continue until the root cause is identified. Use consensus to complete then tidy up the diagram by removing notes and writing-in agreed causes.

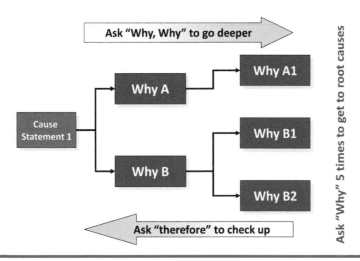

Figure 6.18   **The Why-Why process of verifying answers.**

Outcomes from a Why-Why Analysis should be simple and actionable – if not, then check the process. Seek help and feedback if needed. It is worth spending the time to get to the real root cause (Figure 6.18).

When brainstorming reasons why, it is sometimes helpful to ask:

1. What happens in other departments?
2. Can the solutions be implemented quickly?
3. Is there more than one solution?

The key is to not just accept your first idea, keep delving deeper and if necessary after you have identified a possible cause, go and see if it really is a cause. If you can't identify a root cause then the following table may be helpful.

Challenge	Possible Action
Cause too big and complex to action	You may not have reached the root cause – keep asking why
Can't go any further with causes	If your action is small, specific, and easily actionable, you have probably got far enough
I can't action all these causes	Use data to prioritise actions and identify the key causes. Can you test some easily?
I'm stuck and don't know how to progress	Never give up! 'Go and see' the problem again. Who has experience in this area? Who can you talk to?

4.6 *Verify Each Answer to a* Why *with Data or Observational Evidence*

As you populate the Why-Why Diagram you will need to verify each answer. For example, in the Case Study when asking the first *why* regarding the rack being defective, there were three possible answers: Plates defective due to build-up of rust or foreign material so the paver would not sit correctly, rack plate supports defective so the plate doesn't set exactly flat and firm on the rack, or the rack itself is vibrating. Only by doing a thorough inspection of the plates and the rack supports could these answers be verified or deleted.

4.7 Summarise the Root Cause Pathways that Will Best Address the Problem

Link the answers to your *why* questions so that you have a pathway that will address the problem once acted upon. Again, you should be asking 'what data or observational evidence' do you need to gather to verify this is the best pathway to follow? The causes on the Why-Why Diagram should be simple and clearly actionable (Figure 6.19).

4.8 Identify Possible Solutions to Each Cause in the Two Pathways

We have found it useful to move the two pathways onto a table that can be inserted into your A3 Summary Sheet.

Without the discipline of asking *why* at least five times and tracking the answers on a Why-Why Diagram, often what happens is a symptom will be addressed rather than the root cause as demonstrated by Cause Statement 1 situation in Figure 6.20, where the defective racks could be repaired with everyone thinking the problem has been addressed, then sometime later the problem returns because of the buckled and moving rails.

4.9 Select All the Solutions You Can Work On

Depending on resource and financial boundaries, select the solutions you wish to take and present to the Daily Review Meeting that initiated the Frontline Problem-Solving Root Cause Analysis for approval to proceed. Highlighting the solutions in bold is a good way of showing others what your intentions are.

4.10 Select All the Remaining Solutions You Can Recommend to Others

Sometimes there may be suggested solutions that are outside the control of the person conducting the Frontline Problem-Solving Root Cause Analysis, however they may be good recommendations. In the case study example regarding Cause Statement 2 and the research and development (R&D) trials, there is a recommendation to the R&D Team highlighted in blue as the production people believe the Classic paver, being the largest paver, may be more susceptible to crumbling or movement if the rack is not running smoothly.

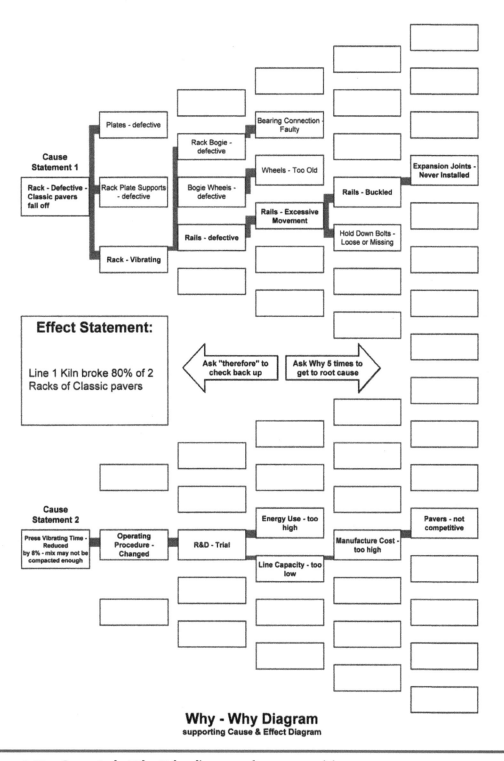

Figure 6.19   Case study Why-Why diagram after summarising.

Final comments regarding Why-Why Analysis

It appears deceptively easy; however, it is very dependent on asking the 'right' questions and exploring the answers. It also tends to imply 'linear' thinking – however some problems are more complex; for example, more than one root cause from different sources. As such having an experienced facilitator can be of great benefit as your people learn and gain their experience.

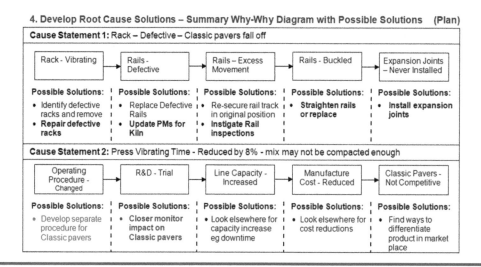

Figure 6.20 **Case study Step 4 summary Why-Why diagram with possible solutions.**

Step 5: Implement Solutions

Now that we have identified the root causes, we need to develop and implement an action plan to permanently fix them.

Action plans should be simple and focused on the short term. We should also be asking – what are the opportunities for mistake proofing to eliminate human error?

Remember – if your action is ineffective or you are unsure where to place the action, then your Root Cause Analysis may be flawed in some way!

There are seven actions which should be completed when implementing solutions:

Step #	Actions
5.1	Establish appropriate criteria for developing solutions
5.2	Identify and select the most appropriate solution or solutions
5.3	Develop a list of proposed key actions for each solution
5.4	Gain approval or permission including all sign-offs required to implement the proposed actions
5.5	Obtain the necessary resources to complete the proposed actions within the required timeframe
5.6	Identify the remaining gaps to achieve the agreed expectation once the initial actions have been completed
5.7	Test or measure the effectiveness of the actions in the short term

5.1 Establish Appropriate Criteria for Developing Solutions

The aim is to identify the root cause and implement some form of corrective action to eliminate it; however, it is the solution that makes the cause go away. Hence, it is important to develop solutions that meet some appropriate criteria:

■ Prevent reoccurrence so it does not happen again for the same set of (known) causes;
■ Be within your control as it is normally easier to enact solutions over which you have control rather than solutions that require other people doing things differently; and
■ Meeting your goals and objectives
  – Does not cause unacceptable problems;
  – Prevents similar occurrences even at different locations; and
  – Provides reasonable value for the cost.

Often it is helpful to refer to the Hierarchy of Controls covered in Figure 6.10 in Step 2 to ensure the proposed solutions are at the best control level.

Select actions over which you have control – don't just delegate everything or enter it into the site's action database.

Be realistic about resources when selecting items to action – don't over commit.

If appropriate, use a simple prioritisation matrix to help select the most appropriate actions for implementation.

5.2 Identify and Select the Most Appropriate Solution or Solutions

To select the solutions you will need to use your Why-Why Diagram or the table you created to insert in your A3 Summary Sheet (refer to Section 4.8 in this chapter).

1. Start on righthand side of the diagram or table;
2. Confirm why the cause is there;
3. Review the possible solutions listed below the cause and identify possible actions that meet your criteria to remove, change or control the cause so that the original problem does not occur;
4. Continue to move to the left, repeating the process; and
5. Evaluate solutions against SMART or Specific, Measurable, Achievable, Realistic and Timely criteria.

SMART actions help ensure that your recommendations are able to be implemented and sustainable (Figure 6.21).

You may find other causes that can be added to the Why-Why Diagram during this process.

Move quickly – don't get bogged down trying to find a solution for each cause.

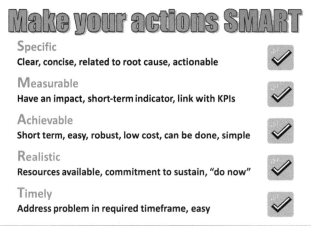

Figure 6.21   **Outline of SMART actions.**

If we refer back to our previous example of Cause Statement 2 press vibrating time – reduced by 8% – mix may not be compacted enough.

Cause Statement 2	*1. Why*	*2. Why*	*3. Why*	*4. Why*	*5. Why*
Press Vibrating Time – Reduced by 8% – mix may not be compacted enough	Operating Procedure – Changed	R&D – Trial	Line Capacity – to low	Manufacture Cost – too high	Pavers – not competitive
Possible Solutions	• Develop separate procedure for Classic pavers	• **Closer monitor impact on Classic pavers**	• Look elsewhere for capacity increase eg downtime	• Look elsewhere for cost reductions	• Find ways to differentiate product in marketplace

A possible practical action that the Production Supervisor could implement is highlighted in red, recognising that addressing the root cause (find ways to differentiate product in marketplace) is outside his boundaries, and more than likely does not provide short-term relief of the problem.

When selecting solutions, we have found it helpful to try to avoid actions like:

■ Re-train only;
■ Punish;
■ Reprimand;
■ Replace the broken part;
■ Investigate;
■ Put up a warning sign;
■ Ignore it – it happens!
■ Revise the procedure without operator involvement;
■ Write a new procedure without operator involvement;

If one of the above solutions is put forward you may not be 'preventing recurrence' and as such you should investigate your solution again.

Also, beware of push solutions – top down fixes that are implemented without adequate involvement of the people affected. Push solutions can be difficult to maintain unless they:

- Address a significant safety issue;
- Remove an issue or stop an action;
- Address operator frustrations and are easy to sustain; and
- Involve an engineering fix with high level automated mistake proofing.

Solutions such as training only, procedure update, workplace layout issues, or operator interface should be avoided unless there is good engagement of the people involved so they have ownership to the solution.

Implementing a push solution may not be appropriate when dealing with people issues. If a solution requires management effort to enforce and is not self-regulating, then the amount of effort required to sustain it may make it impractical.

Investigate opportunities for mistake proofing and visual controls rather than writing a procedure, as it is often more effective to change the workplace layout or process to support the correct activities rather than to create instructions for people to behave differently (Figure 6.22).

Mistake proofing reduces reliance on procedures, signs, and other administrative controls by making the process impossible to get wrong and the potential problems visible.

Other examples include visual line markings, specially designed gauges and tools, etc. In modern cars you cannot start the car unless your foot is on the brake (auto) or clutch (manual), or you cannot remove the key from the ignition until you put the car into park (auto).

its about making it

You can't shut a smoke alarm unless you have the battery installed correctly

Visual control and barrier stops big kids from getting in the playground

Figure 6.22   **Examples of mistake proofing.**

If we are constrained with the equipment (can't modify it in any real way), we may need to consider visual controls supported by one point lessons (training) that we can easily implement.

5.3 Develop a List of Proposed Key Actions for Each Solution

For each of your selected solutions, develop a list of key proposed actions that are SMART. Identify who will be responsible to undertake these proposed actions and with them determine a realistic timeframe for the completion of these actions. Where possible try to ensure the proposed actions lead to a mistake proof solution. If not, what other solutions can you come up with that will minimise human error when being applied?

5.4 Gain Approval or Permission Including All Sign-Offs Required to Implement the Key Actions

Identify what special sign-offs and other permissions are necessary to gain approval for your proposed actions. Arrange to give a presentation to your Daily Review Meeting that allocated the Frontline Problem-Solving Root Cause Analysis or your manager to ensure agreement and approval to proceed. Your partially completed A0-sized laminated Frontline Problem-Solving Root Cause Analysis A3 Summary Sheet will be very useful to support your presentation.

5.5 Obtain the Necessary Resources to Complete the Proposed Actions within the Required Timeframe

■ What equipment or tools will be required to implement the proposed actions?
■ What personnel will you require to undertake, support or supervise the proposed actions?
■ Are all personnel available to undertake the proposed actions they are responsible for?
■ Are all your resources available to be applied or called-upon within your proposed timeframe? If not, re-adjust your proposed timing of the actions.

5.6 Identify the Remaining Gaps to Achieve the Agreed Expectation Once the Initial Actions Have Been Completed

■ What are the implementation results of the initial actions?
■ How can you be sure that these initial actions are achieving the required expectation?
■ What is the identified gap between the results so far and the required expectation?
■ How will you modify or add to the actions to achieve the required expectations?

5. Implement Solutions – Summary of Action Plan			(Do)
Proposed Actions / Approved Actions	Who	Proposed Date	Completed Date
Undertake risk assessment prior to entering kiln	Mick Barker	12 June	12 June
Inspect all racks including bogies and wheels	Mick Barker	13 June	13 June
Inspect rails in Kiln	Emma Peel	13 June	13 June
Investigate with Engineering the design of the expansion joints	Jo Smith	14 June	14 June
Instigate PM routine for Racks, Bogies and Rails	Bill Brown	15 June	15 June
Install new expansion joints	Jo Smith	16 June	18 June

Figure 6.23   Case study Step 5 summary of action plan.

5.7 Test or Measure the Effectiveness of the Actions in the Short Term

■ What is the best method to test or measure the effectiveness of the actions to date? Involve the relevant experts to help identify the best method.
■ How often should you test or measure to ensure your results are correct?
■ What would be the best frequency of testing or measuring the results?
■ Can you identify a pattern in your results?
■ Have you kept the Daily Review Meeting, managers and stakeholders informed of your progress so far? (Figure 6.23)

Step 6: Evaluate Results

Now that the approved action plan has been implemented, it is time to measure and evaluate the results and lock in the gains. The results should be clear and compelling.

When evaluating the results from your actions, you should consider the following:

■ Have your actions been effective and are there measurable results?
■ Have all further practical refinements been exhausted?
■ Have the gains been locked in to prevent reoccurrence of the problem?

Common observation is that this step is either ignored or done poorly. People get distracted by the 'next problem' and want to move onto it. This is often brought about by a lack of an effective system that ensures that there is complete problem closure.

Common statements we hear and our responses:

Common Statement	Our Response
'We have implemented the actions so therefore we must have fixed it'	Can you prove it?
'We don't have time, as we are too busy fixing the next problem'	Are you prepared for this one to come back again?

There are four actions which should be completed when evaluating results:

Step #	Action
6.1	Ensure your actions are having the required impact
6.2	If appropriate, conduct an acid test
6.3	Lock in the improvements
6.4	Review your containment action

6.1 Ensure Your Actions Are Having the Required Impact

Measure the results and where appropriate ensure results are presented in the same format as you defined your problem, refer to Problem Definition in Step 1. Verify you have the evidence to prove that your actions are having the expected impact. If not, determine what further actions you have to take. If required, seek additional assistance to achieve your desired outcomes.

If your actions are only a trial, consider what needs to be done to support them in the longer term. Review the original analysis to ensure you have truly addressed the causes.

6.2 If Appropriate, Conduct an Acid Test

An acid test is where you reintroduce the root cause and see if the problem comes back. If the problem doesn't come back you may not have fixed the right issue. For example in our case study, if we believed the 8% reduction in vibration time caused the Classic pavers (the largest of all the pavers) to be less stable and more susceptible to vibration damage we would introduce the 8% reduction in vibration time for say one rack of Classic pavers followed by a rack with normal vibration time, then monitor if any falls over as they come out of the kiln compared to the normal vibration time rack. If a substantial amount of the reduced vibration time racks fall over and are damaged compared to the normal vibration time racks, it could be concluded we have identified one of the root causes. In some situations, it may not be safe to reintroduce the root cause in which case the acid test would not be used.

If it is feasible and safe to use an acid test to determine the success of the actions implemented, then arrange for such a test.

6.3 Lock in the Improvements

Determine what needs to be done to lock in the improvement to ensure it is sustainable. If appropriate, use mistake proofing to ensure the improvement will always be applied. If there is a need to provide training or update documents to assist in locking in the improvements, ensure such training or document updates are completed to agreed site standards.

6.4 Review Containment of Problem

In Step 2: Contain problem, you may have introduced some temporary measures until you were able to find the root causes and implement appropriate solutions. It is now time to look back on any containment actions to determine whether they were effective and if they can now be removed. It is critical there is good communication of any actions to all those people affected (Figure 6.24).

Step 7: List Future Actions

The aim of Step 7 is to capture the learning to allow the ideas and solutions to be applied elsewhere to similar problems across the organisation.

Once we have solved our problem we should actively look for where this or similar problems may exist elsewhere in the organisation. This is known as Horizontal Deployment.

There are four actions which should be completed when listing future actions:

Step #	Action
7.1	Adjust or refine solutions
7.2	Recommend future actions
7.3	Complete Frontline Problem-Solving Root Cause Analysis A3 Summary Sheet
7.4	Conduct Horizontal Deployment where appropriate

7.1 Adjust or Refine Solutions

Reflect on the solutions we have implement as well as the ones we have recommended. If feasible, take the opportunity to adjust or refine your solutions to ensure they will be sustainable.

This may require re-commencing the P-D-C-A cycle if the desired results have not been achieved. It may require locking in the solutions by updating work

6. Evaluate Results – Measure and evaluate the results of the improvements made (Check)

Rails in Kiln repaired
Any defective Racks, Bogie or Wheels replaced
Instigated PM routine for Racks, Bogies and Rails
New expansion joints appear effective
Broken pavers per rack now running consistently at less than standard of <2.5%

Figure 6.24   Case study Step 6 measure and evaluate the results.

instructions or methods and standard operating procedures, in addition to conducting training and applying mistake proofing or visual controls.

7.2 Recommend Future Action

There are often loose ends once you have completed your actions that may not be within your control. As such it is important to list these in your future actions so that they can be shared at your Daily Review Meeting and, if deemed appropriate, either added to the meeting action list or to the Parking Lot Escalation List to send up to the High Level Daily Review Meeting or management meeting (Figure 6.25).

7.3 Complete Frontline Problem-Solving Root Cause Analysis A3 Summary Sheet

If you haven't progressively done so, create a softcopy Frontline Problem-Solving Root Cause Analysis A3 Summary Sheet from the A0-sized laminated Cause & Effect Diagram, Why-Why Diagram and A3 Summary Sheet to allow for audit review, sharing and filing.

At this point, if you haven't already done so, have your site's improvement facilitator or coach review your A3 Summary Sheet to ensure the information is easily read and understood, and to the site standard. Hopefully they will also provide feedback on how you can further enhance your problem-solving skills when tackling your next Frontline Problem-Solving Root Cause Analysis.

Present your outcomes using your A0 sized laminated sheets or your softcopy file to the Daily Review Meeting that initiated the Frontline Problem-Solving Root Cause Analysis so that your peers can provide feedback and, if necessary, ideas for making any further adjustments to your A3 Summary Sheet.

If you also used a Frontline Problem-Solving Root Cause Analysis User Workbook, take it along with photos of your Cause & Effect Diagram and Why-Why Diagram and ensure these and any other data collected are filed in a central location so that it is available for future reference.

Most importantly, on the completion of a problem-solving activity, recognise everyone's involvement and contributions and celebrate the success as appropriate (Figure 6.26).

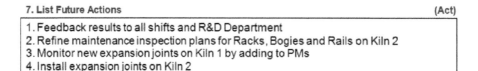

Figure 6.25 **Case study Step 7 list future action.**

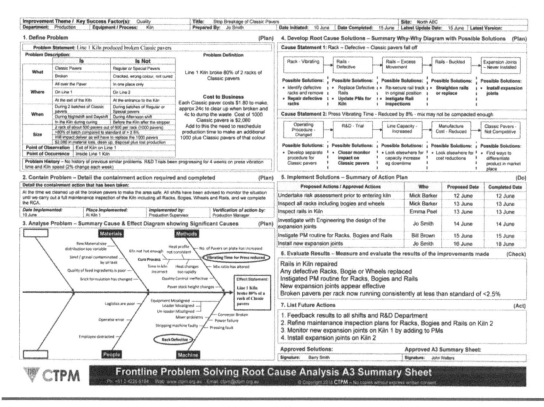

Figure 6.26 Case study Frontline Problem-Solving Root Cause Analysis A3 Summary Sheet.

7.4 *Conduct Horizontal Deployment Where Appropriate*

Horizontal Deployment is about applying the learning from solving this problem to other parts of the organisation. It is more than just telling a few people about what you have done. It's about actively looking and seeking where the ideas and solutions that you have come up with can be applied elsewhere in the organisation.

Horizontal Deployment is very valuable if you have other sites or locations which use similar equipment, processes, hazards, or are in the same environment. It is about identifying other places in your organisation where this problem may occur, or other people who would be interested in the way you have identified and addressed this problem.

Hopefully, if done correctly it will prevent similar problems from happening elsewhere while building on the learning from this problem-solving exercise. It can also save money, time and effort by not having to reinvent the wheel. There may also be some new learning from similar implementations which will make this solution even better.

Examples could include:

■ Applying this improvement to other similar problems on the same machine or process
■ Applying the improvement to similar problems within the business
■ Applying the improvement principles across the organisation

Look in the following places and locations to try and find similar problems

- Same equipment in a different location or site
- Same environment but different equipment
- Similar product
- Similar process or processing steps
- Similar hazards

Reflection on the 7 Step Process

Effective problem solving is also about improving the way that we solve problems. Being able to reflect on the problem-solving process and consider improvement opportunities will help to develop problem solvers. The following questions are often helpful to identify lessons and learning from applying the 7 Step Process to Frontline Problem-Solving Root Cause Analysis:

- What went well?
- What could have gone better?
- What would you do differently next time?
- What were some of the major achievements and breakthroughs that you had?

Key Learning from Frontline Problem-Solving Root Cause Analysis

The best way to create an environment for the on-going Frontline Problem-Solving Root Cause Analysis development of your people is to have them, once properly trained through a suitable development program, involved in Frontline Problem-Solving Root Cause Analysis at least 5% of their normal work time each week, while you continue to have events or incidents that will impact achieving your daily performance expectations.

Another means to further develop your people is to have them involved in addressing simple pro-active improvement opportunities using the mini micro problem-solving 7 Step Process which is based on a similar user workbook and the same tools as the Frontline Problem-Solving Root Cause Analysis (Figure 6.27).

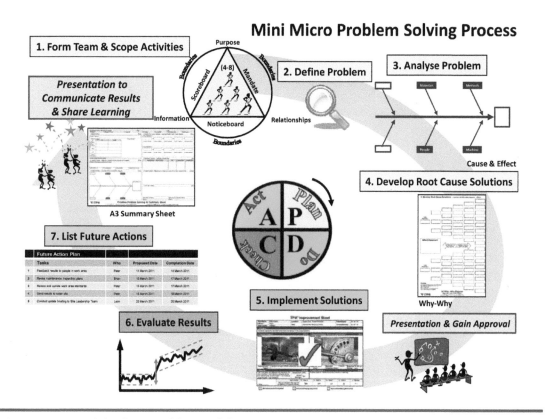

Figure 6.27 Mini micro problem-solving process.

Chapter 7

Rapid Sharing of Learning Capability – Element 7

The Need for a Learning Organisation

Over the years successful businesses have continued to find ways to have a competitive advantage in the marketplace. Competitive advantage can come from a number of business areas including unique products and services, unique distribution channels and methods, unique financing, and operational capability.

What Toyota has demonstrated to the world with their Toyota Production System is that operational capability is one of the hardest competitive advantages to replicate quickly and easily as compared to products and services, distribution channels and methods or financing.

Historically, competitive advantage from Operational Capability has evolved over the years. Back in the 1950s and 1960s as shown in Figure 7.1, it was being the lowest cost producer that gave you a competitive advantage in the marketplace. Those businesses that could not compete on cost soon faded away or were taken over by more successful businesses.

The awareness of the Toyota Production System became apparent in the early 1980s with publication of books like *Japanese Manufacturing Techniques* by Richard Schonberger, and Productivity Press releasing many Japanese translated books on the tools of quality. There became a groundswell for the quality movement with Total Quality Control and Total Quality Management becoming the buzz terms as businesses realised that if they could be the lowest cost producer with the highest quality they would have an extra competitive advantage.

The steelworks in Port Kembla had a foundry area that produced iron castings using very old technology called cupola furnaces. This was fine in the 1970s when the maintenance departments just ordered 'grey cast iron' casting; however, in the 1980s when quality became the focus and quality standards were established, customers or maintenance departments no longer wanted 'grey cast iron' but rather cast iron to an ISO standard. As such the cupola furnaces had to go and were replaced by induction furnaces which allowed much greater metallurgical control when producing molten metal.

Over the next decade everyone worked hard at getting their quality up, still staying cost competitive, while those that didn't make the transition faded away or were taken over.

In the mid-1980s the Just-in-Time movement came along as businesses realised that being responsive to the marketplace while still having high quality and low costs could provide a competitive advantage. The advantage for their customers was that they didn't have to hold large amounts of inventory as the lead time from order to delivery was significantly reduced, while still providing high quality and low cost. Also, if they wanted something and the quality and cost was the same but one supplier could deliver in half the time, then they were the one to get the order. Again, over the next decade those who embraced this new operational capability thinking went well and those who didn't or couldn't soon faded away or were taken over.

In the mid-1990s the innovation movement came along. Marketing realised that the customer was more enlightened and informed, and wanted something a little different. Often this had to do with the packaging rather than the product itself, such as redesigning the shape of the bottle or packet, or adding an extra 20% as a bonus. This had significant ramifications for operations as the number of SKUs or Stock Keeping Units increased, set-up and changeovers to different SKUs become critical and overall complexity increased. Again, over the next decade those who embraced this new operational capability of being able to do small batches with minimal changeover times and applying Green Stream scheduling through flow logic, went well as they maintained or enhanced their responsiveness, quality and costs; however, those who didn't or couldn't soon faded away or were taken over.

Since the mid-2000s we have a new focus in operations called learning. With all the changes occurring with products and processes during the innovation phase, we needed to be capable of rapidly updating everyone of all changes taking place, not to mention the learning as the changes are implemented. As

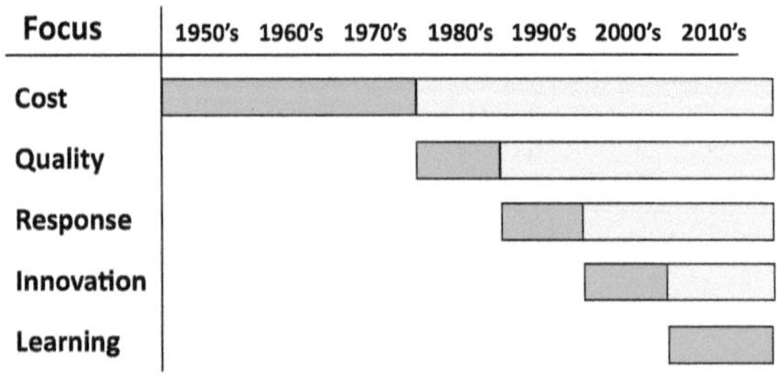

Figure 7.1   **Business trends to achieve competitive advantage.**

such the new operational capability competitive advantage is about being able to rapidly share learning.

> At one site that went through the innovation phase mentioned above, they found their food products became very popular overseas and there was an opportunity to rapidly expand their range for a growing export market. However, their biggest barrier was the ability to communicate all the changes to their workforce which worked a 12-hour roster pattern of 2 days, 2-nights then 4 days off. While people were away for four days there could be quite a number of changes to product specifications and packaging requirements. One of their early solutions was to move the workforce back to 8 hour shifts so they worked 5 days on and 2 days off. They also introduced Effective Daily Management and an improvement knowledge base linked to their equipment structure to allow the storage of all improvement outcomes including their Frontline Problem-Solving Root Cause Analysis A3 Summary Sheets to facilitate easy sharing of the learning.

Actions to Help Create a Learning Organisation

Establish Standards for Documenting Outcomes

One of the keys to rapid sharing of learning is to document outcomes to agreed standards so that everyone can quickly and easily understand information being presented. The agreed standards could relate to where you display information on a board, the way you display your measures such as using coloured bar charts for weekly measures and run charts for daily trends. Agreed standards could relate to the language used in your Frontline Problem-Solving Root Cause Analysis A3 Summary Sheets like describing the variables or potential causes in the Cause & Effect Diagram using the 'object-deviation' format.

As such there should be a site standard for creating all A3 Summary Sheets especially the Frontline Problem-Solving Root Cause Analysis A3 Summary Sheets so that they are easy to understand by anyone. There should also be a sign-off process in place that ensures all A3 Summary Sheets are reviewed by a designated person responsible for the A3 Summary Sheet site standard or standards, so that they can coach the creator of each sheet in understanding and applying the appropriate standard.

Establish a Continuous Improvement Library and Knowledge Base

If something is in a familiar format and easy to read (no jargon, etc.) people can refer to it providing it is easily accessible. This is why having a physical improvement library and a computerised improvement knowledge base established is also critical. Often sites will use the Equipment Structure model used by maintenance to set up their improvement library and knowledge base so that when an incident occurs such as a quality problem or breakdown on a machine or in an area, it is easy to refer to the improvement library or knowledge base for any previous Frontline Problem-Solving Root Cause Analysis A3 Summary Sheets or Improvement Sheets while also cross referencing any maintenance history.

> *Assessment sheet* (Table 7.1) *to help determine whether an adequate and effective physical improvement library and computerised improvement knowledge base been established?*

Establish an Effective Daily Review Meeting Plan

A well thought out Daily Review Meeting plan for a site should be another means to ensure rapid sharing of learning. For example, by having the Frontline Leader conduct their Daily Review Meeting at the start of their shift, then the Frontline Leader attends their Level 1 Daily Review Meeting say 1 hour later they are able to rapidly share learning from their crew with other Frontline Leaders and the support people present.

In developing the site's Daily Review Meeting Plan attention needs to be given when Support Departments conduct their review meetings. At one site we had the local area maintenance person attend the Area Level 1 Production Daily Review Meeting; however, on Fridays he wasn't available because his manager conducted his weekly review meeting with all the maintenance people at the site. Once this was realised, adjustments were able to be made to the timing of both meetings to ensure he was able to attend both meetings with time to spare between them (Figure 7.2).

Create the Right Environment to Promote Adult Learning

We need to be very conscious of the way adults learn, then create an environment in the workplace to allow this to occur on an on-going basis.

In a very simplistic way, adults learn through the process of:

■ Education – understanding why and how;
■ Demonstration – being able to copy;
■ Practice – experience through doing; and
■ Reflection – locking in the learning.

The key is to keep repeating this cycle recognising adults often do not learn new skills and habits by a single training session or improvement event.

The best analogy we have come across regarding proven adult learning techniques is learning to play a musical instrument. When people first take up

Table 7.1   Improvement Library & Knowledge Base Assessment Sheet

Improvement Library & Knowledge Base Assessment Sheet							
Site: Assessor: Date:	Rating Legend 0 – No evidence of activity or 0% 1 – Attempted but no results or 10% 2 – Little evidence of activity or 25% 3 – Half-way to full implementation or 50% 4 – Close to full implementation or 75% 5 – Fully implemented or 100%						
Activity Description	**0**	**1**	**2**	**3**	**4**	**5**	**Comments**
1. There is a clearly defined and centralised physical place (e.g. CI Library) where hard copy CI support materials (e.g. CI training manuals, CI Team outcomes, reference books, etc.) are located							
2. The concept of 'a place for everything and everything in its place' has been applied to the CI library							
3. Where applicable, visual controls have been applied to the CI library to make it easy to locate all CI support material							
4. All personnel know about the CI library and they have access to it							
5. There is a procedure established for requesting/returning CI support material							
6. An effective computerised CI knowledge base that is accessible by all personnel and is up to date (e.g. latest version forms etc.) has been established to support the CI journey at the site							
7. Mid-way and final Team presentations, pre-cycle strategy outcomes, A3 Summary Sheets, Improvement Sheets, One Point Lessons, Team Records etc. are logically filed (soft copy) in the CI knowledge base to support existing and future CI activities							
8. Where applicable the computerised CI knowledge base is structured based on the site's equipment structure (especially storage of A3 Summary Sheets and Improvement Sheets)							
9. All personnel know about the computerised CI knowledge base and they have access to it							
10. All personnel effectively use the computerised CI knowledge base and CI library and benefit from them							
Totals:							**Total/50** **X 2 = %**

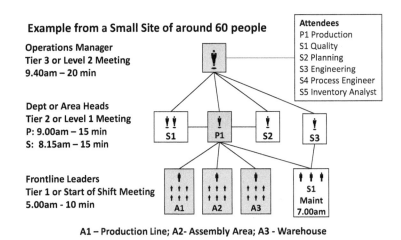

Figure 7.2   Developing an Effective Daily Management plan so as to support rapid sharing of learning.

learning a musical instrument they typically start from a very low skill level with the instrument, which leads onto the following question:

> *Is it better to have a 2 or 3 day intensive lesson on how to play a musical instrument or have a half-hour lesson each week over several years with regular practice and encouragement in order to become competent in playing the musical instrument?*

The answer is obvious in that regular lessons over a period of time, is a well proven adult learning method. This thinking underpins *on-going improvement* mentioned in the Introduction under Pro-active Improvement. It is where people spend up to 5% of their normal work time each week involved in strategically driven Continuous Improvement Teams that typically span up to 12–14 weeks before concluding, celebrating then starting again.

Effective Daily Review Meetings are a great opportunity to develop not only your leaders but all your people each day by introducing or re-enforcing learning at each meeting.

This leads to another often-used question:

> *Is it better to train and develop your people and maybe have them leave, or not train and develop your people and have them stay?*

Chapter 8

The Way Forward

One of the biggest challenges we find at many sites is to get management to recognise the need for doing something about improving daily management. Often the site manager and their team are too busy doing new projects and responding to initiatives from corporate that developing Effective Daily Management gets little attention.

At one site we came across, when engaged by corporate to assist in introducing and implementing TPM (Total Productive Maintenance) & Lean, the site manager had handed the responsibility of developing and conducting a site Daily Review Meeting to the Improvement Co-ordinator. Even though all the intentions were good, not having any line authority meant the Improvement Co-ordinator struggled to get any traction, let alone any enthusiasm from the attendees.

We have also seen the situation where corporate developed a daily management process with supportive fancy information boards and imposed it onto their many sites only to end up with what we would term 'compliance meetings', which were of little value to the attendees or the site.

So the question becomes, How best should we go forward to review and enhance our Daily Review process?

First, we would suggest getting the Management Team at the site to recognise the importance of Effective Daily Management at all levels or tiers. This sounds very obvious however, as mentioned earlier, at many sites we have found management to be so busy with improvement initiatives and corporate compliance issues that they don't see the importance of Effective Daily Management. They think that the current, often ineffective, start of shift and morning meetings being conducted are sufficient.

Preparation Action Plan

Recognising the importance of Effective Daily Management can be assisted by having the Site Management Team complete the Daily Management Innocence to Excellence Rating Sheet from the Introduction. This also provides a baseline before introducing any changes to current practices.

Once they are on board, the next action would be to have the Management Team confirm or establish the site's Key Success Factors for Operations as outlined in Chapter 3, and determine the order they are to be presented.

Once you have your Key Success Factors for Operations model for the site, all the existing site performance measures should be displayed under the relevant Key Success Factor in a consistent presentation format. If there are gaps in what is currently being reported then such gaps should be addressed by the appropriate manager.

If it is an issue, conduct a review of the organisation structure including the role of your Frontline Leaders to ensure there will be clear ownership and accountability as outlined in Chapters 1 and 2.

Finally from a preparation perspective, create a Daily Review Meeting Plan by determining the number of Daily Review Meetings required at each level or tier including support departments, and the most appropriate times for all the meetings (Figure 8.1).

We have found a team-based approach including the key people involved in the Daily Review Meeting is the best way to obtain good buy-in and ownership to the process. As such we suggest you select at least two meetings from your Daily Review Meeting Plan as a trial or pilot. As highlighted in Chapter 4, the development process starts at the top and works down your organisation structure so we would suggest starting with the top level (Tier 4 or Level 3 if a large site or Tier 3 or Level 2 if a small site) and at least one of the

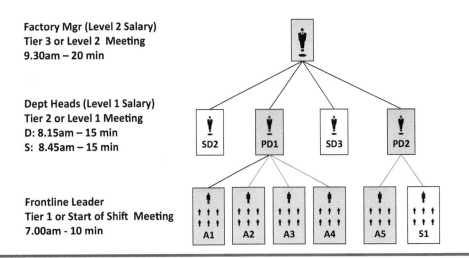

Figure 8.1   **Example daily review meeting plan at a small site of about 80 people. Note: Level 1 Production Department (PD) meetings are at a different time to Support Department (SD) meetings so Support people can attend the Production meeting**

teams at the next level down (Tier 3 or Level 2 for a large site and Tier 2 or Level 1 for a small site).

Implementation Action Plan

For each pilot Daily Review Meeting selected, establish a Cross-functional Improvement Team with 5–8 key attendees and have the person responsible for the Daily Review Meeting lead the team. Some companies also have a higher level or tier person such as a member of the Site Management Team, be a team member to provide support and guidance to the team.

Next step would be to form teams and provide education to each team either separately or combined on what is best practice for Daily Review Meetings; have them rate the site's performance and their performance using the rating sheets from the Introduction and at the end of this Chapter. We have found this is best done using a 4 hour or two 2 hour kick-off workshops where the team can be formed and have what is expected of them explained. We have found creating a Team Information Sheet before setting up an Improvement Team can be very helpful to minimise any ambiguity in what is expected. This also allows the Site Management Team to buy-in and sign-off on it before presenting to the team (Table 8.1).

Key tasks for the improvement teams would be to establish their Daily Review Meeting agenda, design up their Information Centre and start conducting their Daily Review Meetings. It is the doing part that brings out the learning. It is not uncommon to change at least one performance measure every week as the teams realise what is important, especially when reporting different events that happen within their area along the way.

As the run charts are populated from your daily performance scoreboard you start to see trends and issues that may not have been so obvious beforehand.

It is very much an exercise of making enhancements, monitoring their impact, then reflecting on what further changes are required over the following month or so. Once everyone is comfortable with progress then introducing Frontline Problem-Solving Root Cause Analysis should be considered. Often this is a recommendation from the improvement team after they have completed their cycle and made a final presentation to the site's Management Team. At this stage the site may consider introducing a Frontline Problem-Solving Root Cause Analysis Development Plan as outlined in Chapter 6. Once the development plan is completed the Information Centres would need to be updated to include the initial Root Cause Analysis triggers and policies supported by a Root Cause Analysis Action List. an action list The triggers and policies should be reviewed at least every 3 months if not earlier along with reviewing the targets for all the daily performance measures.

Table 8.1 **Example Team Information Sheet for a Daily Review Process Improvement Team**

Team Information Sheet				
Date:			Focus Area:	Production
Reason for Selection:	Need to establish an effective Daily Management Process to review our daily performance to expectations, and to allow issues and problems to be identified at the earliest possible time and then actioned so that they don't happen again			
Mandate:	• Establish an effective Daily Review Process for Tier 2 or Level 1 Daily Review Meeting, then Tier 1 or Start of Shift Meetings in agreed areas • Establish appropriate visually controlled Information Centres that allows holistic reporting by the relevant leaders and ensures any deviations from pre-determined expectations of performance can be identified and rapidly addressed with sustainable corrective actions • Achieve a score of at least 80% on the Daily Review Meeting Rating Sheet • Recommend and prioritise any further improvement opportunities • Complete within 10 team weeks			
Boundaries:	**Physical:**	Within the defined focus area		
	Technology:	No change to existing technology unless approved		
	Team Resources:	Use existing resources, any extra resources to be approved by Management Time for meetings per week: up to 1.5 hours; Time for support activities per week: 1.0 hour		
	Financial:	All improvement activities must be cost-benefit justified and funded within the company's delegation of authority and its current business plan		
Starting	**Daily Management I to E Rating: TBA**		**Target**	**Daily Management I to E Rating: Improve by 25%**
	Daily Review Meeting Rating: TBA			**Daily Review Meeting Rating: +80%**

Checklist for Developing an Effective Daily Management Process				
	#	Action	Comments	✓
Preparation	1	Complete the Daily Management Innocence to Excellence Rating Sheet to create a baseline of your current situation		
	2	Confirm or establish the site's Key Success Factors for Operations, the order for them to be presented and the site performance measures to be reported under each Key Success Factor		

(Continued)

Table 8.1 (Continued)   Example Team Information Sheet for a Daily Review Process Improvement Team

	#	Action	Comments	✓
	3	Establish the site standard for displaying performance measures		
	4	Review current organisation structure in light of ownership and responsibility at all levels, and determine any actions required, and any constraints to be considered, regarding the personnel who will be attending Daily Review Meetings		
	5	Create a Daily Review Meeting Plan by determining the number of Daily Review Meetings required at each level or tier including support departments, and the most appropriate times for all the meetings		
	6	Select at least 2 pilot Daily Review Meetings to demonstrate to the rest of the site		
Implementation	7	Establish a Cross-functional Improvement Team of 5–8 key attendees covering at least production, maintenance, planning and despatch		
	8	Conduct a half-day Daily Management Process workshop followed by a series of follow-up (suggest weekly) meetings of 1-hour duration to plan and monitor progress of activities (typically 8 meetings)		
	9	Establish an effective Daily Review Meeting Agenda		
	10	Create an effective Daily Review Meeting Information Centre		
	11	Educate everyone involved, and commence the new Daily Review Meetings		
	12	Monitor the effectiveness of the above and refine as required (over 2–4 weeks)		
Lock-in	13	When appropriate, establish initial triggers and policies for Frontline Problem-Solving Root Cause Analysis		
	14	If necessary introduce a suitable Frontline Problem-Solving Root Cause Analysis Development Program		

Daily Review Meeting Rating

Daily Review Meetings should be conducted at each level or tier of operations. Below is a simple 10 Requirements Rating Sheet that can be used to baseline your current situation and evaluate your progress.

Focus of Meeting:	Rating Legend					
Date of Rating:	0 – No evidence of activity or 0%					
Assessor:	1 – Attempted but limited results or 10%					
	2 – Some evidence of activity or 25%					
	3 – Half-way to full implementation or 50%					
	4 – Close to full implementation or 75%					
	5 – Fully implemented or 100%					
Requirements for an Effective Daily Review Meeting	**0**	**1**	**2**	**3**	**4**	**5**
1. The Daily Review Meeting is scheduled each working day at a set time, at a set place and with a set agenda						
2. Meeting always starts on time and finishes on or before time as indicated by clock in room with visual control displayed (e.g. green for time of meeting)						
3. All attendees turn up prepared with the right information every meeting						
4. The meeting agenda is on display, flows in line with the design of the Information Centre, has time allocations for each item, and is always followed						
5. A visual Information Centre covering at least a daily scoreboard for each area represented, daily run charts for the month to monitor trends in performance and action list has been established to support the meeting with all information displayed so that it can be read from at least 2 metres away						
6. The Information Centre (and meeting) is in a location that promotes regular viewing by as many people as practical						
7. The Information Centre is updated before each meeting by the relevant responsible persons and operates to defined visual standards e.g. colour coding, standardisation of reports, with any deviations from expectation highlighted in red so all can see						

8. All tasks generated at meeting are documented on displayed Action Board with date, area, initiator, description of task, person responsible to address, target date and provision for revised date, and comments with progress monitored on a daily basis with changes marked in red						
9. There is a documented policy on display that sets the triggers and rules for instigating Frontline Problem-Solving Root Cause Analysis with the policy always being followed and when appropriate, updated						
10. All attendees leave meeting feeling engaged and with all the information and support they require to achieve the Production or Work Plan for the shift/day						
Number per Column:						
Multiply by:	0	1	2	3	4	5
Score per Column:						
Total/50:						
X 2						%

Reference List of Articles and Books

Articles/Papers

Jim Huntzinger. The Roots of Lean, Training within Industry: The Origin of Japanese Management and Kaizen. Lean Frontiers, 2005.

Ross Kennedy. Understanding the Concepts of Training within Industry and Standardised Work. CTPM – The Centre for TPM & Lean/CI, 2016.

Steven Spear and H. Kent Bowen. Decoding the DNA of the Toyota Production System. *Harvard Business Review*, Sep–Oct 1999.

Books

James P. Womack, Daniel T. Jones, and Daniel Roos. The Machine that Changed the World. Free Press, 1990.

Jeffrey K. Liker. The Toyota Way: 14 Management Principles of the World's Greatest Manufacturer. McGraw-Hill, 2004.

Jeffrey K. Liker. Toyota Talent: Developing your People the Toyota Way. McGraw-Hill Professional Publishing, 2007.

Jeffrey K. Liker and Gary L. Convis. The Toyota Way to Lean Leadership: Achieving and Sustaining Excellence through Leadership Development. McGraw-Hill Education, 2011.

Per Petersson, Björn Olsson, Thomas Lundström, Ola Johansson, Martin Broman, Dan Blücher, and Henric Alsterman. Leadership – Making Lean a Success. Part Media, 2013.

Richard J. Schonberger. Japanese Manufacturing Techniques: Nine Hidden Lessons in Simplicity. Free Press, 1982.

Ross Kenneth Kennedy. Understanding, Measuring and Improving Overall Equipment Effectiveness: How to Use OEE to Drive Significant Process Improvement. CRC Press/Productivity Press, August 2017.

Steven J. Spear. The High Velocity Edge. McGraw-Hill Publishing, 2009.

.

Index

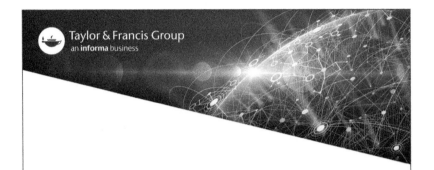